# 42 DAYS
## *to a*
# MORE
# POWERFUL
# PRAYER
# LIFE

# 42 DAYS
## *to a*
# MORE POWERFUL PRAYER LIFE

## A SIMPLE
## 6-WEEK GUIDE

GLENN HASCALL

## BARBOUR BOOKS
An Imprint of Barbour Publishing, Inc.

Published by Barbour Books, an imprint of Barbour Publishing, Inc., P.O. Box 719, Uhrichsville, Ohio 44683, www.barbourbooks.com

*Our mission is to inspire the world with the life-changing messsage of the Bible.*

Member of the
Evangelical Christian
Publishers Association

Printed in the United States of America.

# INTRODUCTION

You're here seeking answers. There is something within everyone that longs to be close to God. But how? When the struggle leaves you feeling discouraged you look for new answers and fresh hope. This book can help define a prayer path that results in a real connection to God. Keep a notebook handy to record your thoughts. A simple method of keeping track of your responses will be to list the page number and then add an "N" for notes, "C" for challenge, and "R" for reflection.

Whether you're walking this prayer journey alone, using this in a small group setting, or are taking one close friend with you, there are questions and answers within the pages that help drive each issue to a place of understanding and belief.

Prayer may seem like a one-sided conversation. There can be times when it seems God is silent. There are answers, and God can, will, and does speak to His family.

Everyone wants answers—God has them. He has a plan for your life, and He's not selfish in withholding that plan. It could be a matter of learning how to ask, how to listen, and how to manage what you learn. He will speak to your need.

The journey starts now. Grab your notebook, turn this page, and uncover the first steps of this week's journey.

# Week 1

## PRAYING FOR OTHERS

*Prayer is the link that connects us with God.*
A. B. Simpson

Fold your hands. Bow your head. Close your eyes.

You probably understand something important is going to happen when you hear these three phrases. You'll talk to God in prayer. It may start with something simple and repetitive, but growth brings a more familiar connection with the One to whom you pray.

Babies experience this when all they can say is "Mama." Mothers will tell their children all kinds of things, but babies can only contribute limited words. The babies don't give up—they learn the language of their parents. Understanding begins.

This is the time to go beyond memorized prayers and words you think you should say, to discover something more personal and meaningful. The Bible is a powerful guide helping you find the heart of prayer. Explore the depths of the ways God connects with you through conversation.

More than formula or method, your time in these pages should be spent learning the importance of prayer and the things God likes to hear about most.

Take those *folded hands, head bowed, and eyes closed moments* and dedicate them to praying for others. It may sound easy. If this were a test, you might think it would be an easy A. You agree—praying for others makes sense. Stay close, pray for wisdom, read carefully. God is asking you to pray for people you never expected. You might feel defensive or wonder if there's a waiver that could get you out of praying this way. You may say, "I'm not ready for this." You might think you signed up for a different course.

You'll confront questions that require personal decisions. Preconceived ideas may be challenged. In the end, you might be better equipped to deal with an inner *bitterness infection* that's caused long-term pain with absolutely no relief. You might discover you're asked to pray for people you don't agree with, or even for those who've hurt you.

Your prayers will come with a benefits package for yourself, and those you pray for. You'll be inviting God to get involved. You'll be asking Him to provide solutions where only problems exist.

Common sense will be challenged because in God's playbook there are things that don't immediately make sense. Where traditional wisdom suggests a restraining order against those who have inflicted pain, God says prayer can change the outcome of your worst experience.

You have an adversary who would love to see you personally take charge of the things you should be praying for. Every moment he can keep you away from God's presence is a greater opportunity to influence your thinking and confuse your decision making.

We're leaving the shore. Get your feet wet. The waters may be familiar—or you may wonder what's below the surface. Dive in. These are healing waters.

# GOD CONVERSATION

*The first thing I want you to do is pray. Pray every
way you know how, for everyone you know.*
1 Timothy 2:1 msg

Conversation. A single word that invites relationship, an exchange of ideas, and the sharing of big dreams. Prayer is only one side of a *God conversation*.

Pray, and God will respond to your prayer conversation through His Word (2 Timothy 3:16), other Christians (Romans 10:17), and the Holy Spirit (John 16:13).

When you speak to God through prayer you get a chance to speak to Him about things that concern you. He doesn't *need* to hear from you to know your concerns, but He still *wants* you to pray, trust, and wait for His answer. Should you expect God to answer prayers you don't pray?

There are reasons deeper than asking God for help that keep Christians praying. Prayers reveal the heart, expose what you really believe, and invite God to take control.

Prayer should be a priority (1 Thessalonians 5:17). You're asked to pray even if you think you're doing it wrong (Romans 8:26). God wants you to pray for everyone you know, even if they're hard to get along with (Matthew 5:44).

Maybe one of the best reasons to pray for someone who gets under your skin is because while the prayer *might* change them, it *will* change you.

Praying for others softens your heart, improves personal compassion, and removes relationship speed bumps.

*Sunday—Morning*

You believe prayer can provide answers to life's greatest challenges. If you didn't, there wouldn't be a need to explore the contents of this book. It may seem odd to begin by praying for others when you're not sure there's any personal benefit. Love is caring enough to meet with a big God about big needs on behalf of other people.

> *Dear God, it's easier to pray for the things I desire than to pray for others. Help me notice the needs of those around me, help them when I can, and pray always. Pull me out of my shell, and help me pay attention to the concerns of those I meet. Amen.*

### CHALLENGE

Think of one person in your family that's hard to pray for—then pray for them.

### REFLECTION

Why is it hard to pray for difficult people?
What stood out to you most in today's reading?

## Sunday—Noon

Praying for others when they're in need can be difficult, especially when you feel they may be getting what they deserve. God wants you to follow His example and show mercy (Luke 6:36). Prayer can be an act of love, a compassionate conversation, and an effective way to decrease personal selfishness.

*Dear God, You make it clear that friends communicate. You've given me Your words to read. Every time I read the Bible I can learn something important about You. If I really care about people I should ask You to help them. When I start praying for personal help, remind me that Your love was offered to every human. Since You care for everyone, help me learn to care for others like You do. Amen.*

### CHALLENGE

When you begin to think of someone who needs more patience than most, consider it a perfect opportunity to pray for them.

### REFLECTION

Can you name three people who cause you to feel annoyed?
Will you pray for their good right now?

## Sunday—Evening

The first full day of this prayer journey is nearing an end. Praying for others can seem less important than praying for your own needs. You might agree that praying for your family is a great idea, but God's command is clear—pray for others, identify with their struggles, help meet their needs.

*Dear God, You don't play favorites. You listen to any family member who prays. You make prayer a way for change to begin. You even ask mature Christians to remember the many reasons to pray. Help me see others with new eyes and maybe even find joy in sharing their burdens in prayer. Amen.*

### CHALLENGE

Think of a neighbor you haven't met yet. Introduce yourself, and then pray for a new friend.

### REFLECTION

How does God respond to people (John 3:16)?
How does compassion change the way you pray for others?

*Week 1: Monday*

# PETITIONS

*Don't fret or worry. Instead of worrying, pray.*
*Let petitions and praises shape your worries into prayers,*
*letting God know your concerns. Before you know it,*
*a sense of God's wholeness, everything coming together*
*for good, will come and settle you down.*

PHILIPPIANS 4:6 MSG

A petition is a formal request made to God. It could be for yourself, but for many Christians a petition is made on behalf of another. Petitions can be a simple request or a gut-wrenching *Without You, help is not coming.*

Prayers transform worry into praise, fear into assurance, and invite God to bring calm into the center of your personal storm. Just think, if God can do that for you, He can do the same for the person you're praying for.

When you pray, you're reminding yourself that the best answers come from God and He's promised to answer. When you pray for others you're essentially saying, "I want God's best for you."

You don't have to go through a ritual, pray a certain prayer, or follow a specific pattern. While these can help, they're not required. You don't have to worry that God won't listen to your prayers just because they differ from the way other people pray.

Petition God for the help others need. He can answer with a yes, no, or wait, but no matter the answer, He always offers grace for each moment (2 Corinthians 12:9–11). When you rejoice, He rejoices with you (Zephaniah 3:17). When things don't turn out the way you wanted, He stays close to the brokenhearted (Psalm 34:18).

*Monday—Morning*

Signing a petition often means you believe something is important enough to take action. You want an issue brought before someone who can make a difference. Petitions even suggest the involvement of many people. Prayer can be that meaningful.

*Dear God, I want to be comfortable enough to petition You on behalf of those You've brought into my life. Help me care enough about those I love to share their concerns with You. Help me never be afraid to ask for the guidance, healing, and grace that others need. Amen.*

### CHALLENGE

Write down five petitions you would like God to answer. Turn this into a prayer.

### REFLECTION

How does thinking of prayer as a petition change the way you think about it?
Does the idea of a petition make your prayer concern seem more or less important? Why?

## *Monday—Noon*

Prayer isn't a competition between Christians, a spiritual sport with trophies for best in show, or something to be critiqued by those with an advanced spiritual vocabulary. God wants to hear your heart. The more time you spend in prayer the more you'll be comfortable praying.

> *Dear God, help me not be intimidated when I hear others pray. Help me also never think I'm better than others when I pray. May my conversation with You be about more than technique and the pursuit of brownie points. May I be more impressed by You so I don't feel the need to try to impress You. Amen.*

### CHALLENGE

Remember that prayer is a personal conversation and not a spiritual performance. Think about the way you speak to others and the ways you may have made a conversation with God different.

### REFLECTION

Why do you think it's easy to compare your ability to pray (positively or negatively) with others'?

Do you think God is more interested in the specific words you use when praying or the heart behind the prayer? Why? Heart

*Monday—Evening*

Today you probably experienced stress and anxiety. Your internal emotion switch might have moved to "freak out" mode. Prayer can be the key to dialing back the anxiety because it puts your focus back on the God who actually is in control. Remember the verse today (see page 12). This would be a great opportunity to *reshape*. Give it a try.

> *Dear God, move my heart back from the brink of falling apart. Hear my cry from the edge of confusion and bring sense to what I can't control. Help me remember You're greater than my personal fear trophies. You're greater than my anxiety collection. You're my greatest source of stress relief. Help me refuse to focus on my own concerns so completely that I can't see the needs of others. Amen.*

### CHALLENGE

Remember that when your adversary, the devil, can successfully get you to focus on yourself, then you'll forget to pray for others. You won't even be able to see their needs.

### REFLECTION

God

What's the connection between praise and stress relief? How can praying for others reduce personal worry?

Shows God you care

*Week 1: Tuesday*

# GOD'S HANDCRAFTED PLAN

*We haven't stopped praying for you, asking God to give you wise minds and spirits attuned to his will, and so acquire a thorough understanding of the ways in which God works.*
COLOSSIANS 1:9 MSG

God isn't held back by your opinion. He does things His own way, and His way is perfect. Where you want step-by-step guides to deal with virtually everything in your life, God handcrafts a plan that is unique to every single individual and circumstance.

Instead of telling God how He should handle another person, pray that other people will be wise in understanding God's plan.

Don't give God an intelligence report on the people you pray for. You may feel like you need to let God know about their past as if He's uninformed, ask Him to be tender toward them because of circumstances they've endured, or tell God about troublemakers in their lives.

God accepts these kinds of prayers because they're filled with compassion for someone He loves, but His plan isn't put aside because you're concerned that the person you're praying for won't be treated fairly.

God knows you better than you know yourself, has greater compassion for people than you'll ever have, and understands exactly what happens next. Maybe that's why God's *better prayer* idea invites you to keep praying and requesting wisdom for your friends. When God works in their life, pray they would have some understanding of what He's doing.

This type of response demands you trust God with the outcome and give your friends to His plan, and suggests that you wait to see God's praiseworthy exclamation point at the end of this crisis chapter.

## Tuesday—Morning

Praying for others is incredibly important in relationships with God, friends, and family. Trust will be required—and God can be trusted. Praying for others can be hard because it removes you from control. God has a plan and it includes you, but when you give God the opportunity to intervene, He can—He does—He will. Stand back. Watch Him work.

*Dear God, You know the story of everyone I'll ever meet. You see behind the pain, the smiles, and the tears. Because I don't know what You know, please help me allow You to work in their lives the way You need to. It may be easy to try to fix people, but that's Your job. Amen.*

### CHALLENGE

Pray that other people will learn wisdom from the Most-Wise, understanding from the Knows-All, and have spirits in tune with the Master-Planner.

Have you ever questioned the way God deals with people
you pray for?

What have you learned today that challenges your thinking?

*Tuesday—Noon*

You can try to be in control or you can allow God to
redirect circumstances. The biggest difference between
these approaches is that God knows the future. You don't.
Pray, and never stop praying. Care, and never stop caring.
Wait, and keep waiting for God's answer.

*Dear God, when I'm impatient, remind me that You control
what I worry about. When I think I have an idea that
fixes issues in others' lives, remind me that You always have
answers I've never considered. When I am concerned for
friends, remind me that You love them more than I do. Amen.*

### CHALLENGE

If you're reading this at lunchtime and there are other
people around you, pick one person and pray for them—
even if you don't know their name. Write down what
impact (if any) this had on you.

### REFLECTION

What prevents you from trusting God with those you
pray for?

What is one thing that God can do for your friends that
you can't?

## *Tuesday—Evening*

You pray for others because you care. One of the best prayers you can pray puts others in the hands of a restoring God. Your prayer can equip them to understand how God can intervene in their lives. Your prayer can bring them in connection with God's good plan.

> *Dear God, because You sent Your Son to save people it means You're in the business of rescue. Forgive me when I try to do Your job. You want me to cooperate with Your plan, but it has to be Your plan—not mine. When I pray that You would help other people recognize Your wisdom, please help me recognize Your wisdom, too. Amen.*

### CHALLENGE

Love people, trust God. Write down what this means to you.

### REFLECTION

Who has more wisdom? You or God?
Who is more trustworthy? You or God?

# LEARNING FROM
# THE MODEL PRAYER

*"Give us this day our daily bread. And forgive us*
*our debts, as we also have forgiven our debtors."*
MATTHEW 6:11–12 NASB

The Lord's Prayer is probably familiar to you. Reactions tend to be a passionate connection to the words or a visible disconnect (often because the prayer can seem more ritualistic than personal).

For Jesus, this prayer had meaning. There's a lot to think about in just a few verses. For Jesus, this was more than a model prayer; it was a verbal reflection of His human experience.

Jesus had a priority prayer list: remembering that His Father was not of this world, that God's name was honorable, He longed for the arrival of God's kingdom, He wanted God's will to be accomplished, He knew the importance of forgiveness, and He was fully aware that humanity struggled with temptation (Matthew 6:9–13).

The Son of God was not reminding Himself of something He might otherwise have forgotten. He was stating facts, and those facts should be important to all who hear the prayer for the first or the thousandth time.

Today's verse puts context to the content. Jesus didn't say, "Give me this day my daily bread, and forgive my debts." It's possible that's what your mind thinks when you read the verse, but Jesus said, "Give *us* this day—forgive *our* sins." It's important to see that Jesus wanted your prayer language to include others. You aren't just asking God to take care of you. Jesus cared for all. Forgiveness and mercy aren't gifts you should hoard.

As you pray for your own needs, include the needs of others.

### Wednesday—Morning

The things Jesus experienced as a man were combined with the things He knew to be true as the Son of God. The Lord's Prayer reflected the needs of man (food, forgiveness, protection), but it reflected His divine nature (a coming kingdom, honoring His Father, a desire to see God's will accomplished). This prayer was both instructive to us and personal for Jesus. It provides a snapshot of the needs of humanity.

*Dear God, may my prayers be more closely connected with Your desires for others. May my prayers offer the same compassion for the needs of others and my absolute trust in Your plans. May You find honor in my words, mercy in my heart, and compassion on my lips. Amen.*

#### CHALLENGE

Pray the Lord's Prayer, and think about who you consider "us" when you pray. Write their names down and set aside time today to pray specifically for each name on your list.

What's the importance of using "us" and "our" instead of
"me" and mine" in the Lord's Prayer?

What stood out to you in today's reading?

## Wednesday—Noon

There is no end to the needs you see each day. Praying
that God would keep "us" from temptation does a very
important thing. It should keep Christians from feeling
superior. You could pray that God would help keep your
friend from temptation, but by including yourself you are
admitting you need help, too. This is called humility. God
likes to see this trait in His family.

> Dear God, You are the Author of life, and the best stories
> always include more than one person. You placed me here
> to discover friendships and then show Your love to others.
> I can't do that if I think only of myself or think of others as
> inferior. Because I have people I love, help me remember to
> include them in my prayer conversations with You. Amen.

### CHALLENGE

Take the key elements of the Lord's Prayer and write an
original prayer that uses the ideas in a new way.

### REFLECTION

How did today's thoughts challenge your perspective on
the Lord's Prayer?

What do you consider the most comforting part of the
Lord's Prayer?

*Wednesday—Evening*

The humility of Jesus shines through in today's model
prayer. He honored His Father, included others in His
requests, and never once prayed in a way that made Him
seem superior (even though He was and is). Perhaps His
example can set the tone for your next prayer.

*Dear God, Your Word is important. It's like reading*
*Your instructions for life. If prayer is how I talk to You,*
*then let me accept Your Word as Your best response. I can*
*learn more when I read the Bible after prayer. Within*
*those words I can share Your values, love Your people,*
*and thirst to learn from the Founder of prayer. Amen.*

### CHALLENGE

Tonight before you sleep, take what you've learned about
the Lord's Prayer and let it change how you think about
the prayer itself and the One who set the example. Share
something you've learned with someone you're praying for.

### REFLECTION

How can the phrase "Our Father" encourage you as you
pray for others?
Why do you think God wants you to pray for His best in
the lives of those you care about?

# PRAYER FROM A NEW CREATION

*[Jesus said], "You're familiar with the old written law, 'Love your friend,' and its unwritten companion, 'Hate your enemy.' I'm challenging that. I'm telling you to love your enemies. Let them bring out the best in you, not the worst. When someone gives you a hard time, respond with the energies of prayer."*

MATTHEW 5:43–45 MSG

Praying for those who hurt you sounds like a bad idea, doesn't it? By praying for them it seems like you're saying the hurt didn't matter, you're willing to endorse bad behavior, and that you're immune to the actions of others.

Praying for someone who's been mean almost sounds as if God is saying we should just accept verbal punishment from an enemy. There's more to it.

When you receive a negative response from others, you're encouraged to practice the lessons you've learned in your *growing-up* walk with Jesus. He suffered at the hands of violent men and said, "Father, forgive them" (Luke 23:34). He was betrayed by Peter and still gave him an important job (John 21). You're asked to forgive others (Colossians 3:13). That takes prayer.

Praying for people you love can be a fairly easy exercise in faith, but praying for those who hurt you suggests you're making progress in becoming the new creation God intended (2 Corinthians 5:17).

The prayers you offer and the forgiveness you extend

are an equal blend of compassion and g
many of the things God asks, praying for
more about you and your future and less a
person and a past they ruthlessly fractured.

## Thursday—Morning

Love removes barriers in relationships. Prayer gives you the chance to care about people. No wonder God asks you to pray for those whom you might otherwise count as enemies. It's hard to remain angry with someone God wants you to pray for.

*Dear God, You know my heart. You know that praying for someone that hurts me or my family doesn't rank high on my priority list. Even when I don't understand, give me the strength to obey Your command to pray. May my obedience help me understand the freedom in forgiveness. Amen.*

### CHALLENGE

Take a moment to think about someone who has hurt you. Pray for them this morning. Add that person to your prayer list throughout the day, and remind yourself there is always value in doing what God asks.

### REFLECTION

What do you think our world would be like if God instructed us to hate our enemies?
How does hate make things harder for human connection?

## Thursday—Noon

God took something that seemed natural (loving friends) and added an unnatural command (love enemies). He wanted both to be beneficial. He knows that prayer has the greatest potential for turning an enemy into a friend. The more enemies you insist on having the fewer potential friends you'll have to choose from.

*Dear God, before I followed You, I was Your enemy. You did something for me that broke down the walls and allowed me to find a friend in my Creator. Your example proves I may not even like potential friends until I pray for them. Including You in all my relationships is starting to make sense. Amen.*

### CHALLENGE

Think about a personal friendship that is strong today but started out less than ideal. Remember, God can repair what your adversary used to instill anger, inspire distraction, and infuse personal discontent. Write down the areas God has either repaired or needs to repair. Think how you can cooperate with Him.

### REFLECTION

How do you think hating an enemy could keep you from staying close to God?

In what way do you think God's command to love your enemies is more practical than punishment?

## Thursday—Evening

The Bible says that when others give you a hard time, you can use that circumstance to pray for them. Maybe God has been waiting for someone to recognize this person needs His help. Maybe they can begin to recognize their need for a Savior when you stop treating them like an enemy.

*Dear God, help me remember that You want to reach every person with Your love. If they don't see love in me, they may not believe it's really something that's available to them. If they treat You badly, I shouldn't expect something better. Help me remember they are designed for relationship and then never stand in their way of discovering You. Amen.*

### CHALLENGE

Try to see people from God's perspective. The more you can begin to love them as He loves and the more you choose to love, the greater impact God can have on people who need Him. Spend time evaluating whether God's love is the gift you love to share.

### REFLECTION

How does this reading help you see there may be a greater reason to pray for an enemy than you thought? How do you think this kind of prayer can improve all your relationships?

## Week 1: Friday

# PRAYER-FOCUSED LEADERSHIP

*Pray. . .for kings and all who are in authority so that
we can live peaceful and quiet lives marked by godliness
and dignity. This is good and pleases God our Savior, who
wants everyone to be saved and to understand the truth.*

1 TIMOTHY 2:2–4 NLT

At any given moment someone holds political office. You
might not have voted for them. You can think there was
some kind of mistake made and that if God was really
in control He should have prevented that individual from
gaining office.

If you *like* political leaders, pray for them. If you *don't
like* political leaders, pray for them.

The Bible is clear that God is involved in the affairs of
kings and other leaders. Romans 13:1 says, "Let everyone
be subject to the governing authorities, for there is no
authority except that which God has established. The
authorities that exist have been established by God" (NIV).

If you think God can't impact world leaders, consider
Proverbs 21:1 which says, "The king's heart is like a stream
of water directed by the LORD; he guides it wherever he
pleases" (NLT).

God cares deeply about the affairs of mankind. He
can change hearts, direct thinking, and inspire mercy. He
works beyond elections, inside boardrooms, and outside our
comfort zone. He asks you to be a good citizen. He invites

you to pray for those who lead.

Leadership doesn't have to be political, so remember to pray for your boss, the ones in charge at your child's school, and those who lead your church. These leaders have a great responsibility, and God's plan always goes beyond conventional thinking.

## Friday—Morning

You don't have to agree with a leader to pray for them. You don't have to vote for someone to know they need guidance. You don't even have to believe they'll be successful to know that God's plan needs to impact their decisions. From politics to the place where you're employed, prayer can create change in ways a picket line never can.

*Dear God, at times I struggle with decisions made by those in leadership that don't seem to connect with Your Word. I find myself thinking of what it would be like if someone else was in charge. Help me remember that each day I pray, the greater the opportunity for my obedience to lead me to understand You've never lost control. Amen.*

### CHALLENGE

When you think about leadership, consider that your prayers should be that God's will would be accomplished, and not your own agenda. Then take the next step and allow God to conform your actions to His plans.

To what degree do you struggle with the idea of praying
  for leaders? Why?

Why do you think it is so easy to criticize leadership?

*Friday—Noon*

God wants you to pray for your boss. This probably won't
be much of a burden if you get along with your boss and
they make decisions you like. This will be much harder if
you think they're unfair or play favorites. Praying for your
employer forces you to consider the pressures they face
while asking God to help them act wisely.

*Dear God, I have had bosses I've liked and some who weren't
favorites. Praying for them seems unnatural. When I find
myself resisting the decision to ask You to help them, may I
remember that You're a God of mercy and grace. Helping
people is what You do best. If I want a better boss, then
praying for them is the perfect first step. Amen.*

## CHALLENGE

Today, when you think of your boss, ask God to give
them wisdom to manage wisely, treat kindly, and serve
compassionately.

## REFLECTION

Why would it be hard to pray for a tough boss?

Why would it be easier to be critical?

## *Friday—Evening*

Pastors provide leadership in your life. Some sermons can make you angry and you may find yourself upset with your pastor. They might have come to a faulty conclusion or have an opinion that differs from yours. There is wisdom. Your prayers can make it available (James 1:5).

*Dear God, there are times when I think the pastor should be praying for me, but praying for them is part of Your command. Help me remember to pray throughout the week for those who study Your Word to help bring truth to Your people. Change their hearts when needed. Change mine so my life looks more like Yours. Amen.*

### CHALLENGE

Write down five things you appreciate about your pastor. Thank God for each item on your list and then share your gratitude with your pastor.

### REFLECTION

What negative circumstances make it hard to pray for your pastor?

What positive things can you do for your pastor after praying for them?

*Week 1: Saturday*

# AN INVITATION TO CONVERSATION

*Get rid of all bitterness, rage, anger, harsh words,*
*and slander, as well as all types of evil behavior.*
*Instead, be kind to each other, tenderhearted, forgiving*
*one another, just as God through Christ has forgiven you.*
EPHESIANS 4:31–32 NLT

Transparency can lead to compassion. Compassion can lead to prayer. Prayer can lead to healing. It's no wonder why God wants you to pray for others. Did you notice honesty and compassion give prayer room to grow?

This week you've been challenged to think through the reasons God might have for praying for family members, friends, enemies, and leaders. There's a connection between prayer for others and the love we have for them. Both begin with a choice. When you choose to love others you will pray for them. When you choose to pray for others you connect with the compassionate heart of God.

When you pray for people there's more going on than just your request. God can use prayer to restore relationships, draw you to Himself, and help you see others in a way you never have before. It will change the way you act.

If there's a lack of harmony in your home, workplace,

church, or world at large, there is something powerful you can do. Pray. Let it break down walls, build *care connections*, inspire hospitality, and provide the human bond God always has in mind.

If you thought prayer was just an obligation that included your most recent spiritual wish list, keep reading. Your spiritual growth will always be enhanced by keeping in contact with the One who invited you to pray.

### Saturday—Morning

If it feels as if prayer draws attention to issues that seem polarizing and divisive, remember, this feeling simply highlights the problem. Agreeing to pray invites God to become the solution. When you refuse to pray, you may be denying that a problem exists or suggesting you don't think you need God's help.

*Dear God, sometimes I don't pray for others because I think I can handle personal relationships on my own. Please remind me that You still want to use me as part of the answer but that the actual solution comes from You. Thanks for bringing solutions to the issues every person will ever face. Amen.*

#### CHALLENGE

Write down the names of people you'll begin praying for and the reason(s) for the prayer. Add to the list whenever needed. Review the list every few weeks to see how God is working.

Why is it so hard to give God control?
Who should you be praying for today because you're
tired of trying to make things work on your own?

*Saturday—Noon*

Bitterness is a by-product of refusing to pray for someone
who's hurt you. On the other hand, prayer can provide
needed closure because you're placing your hurt in the hands
of the Healer. You may never have a perfect relationship
with that person again, but prayer lances your *soul wound*
and allows the bitterness to leave the wound free from long-
term infection. Let the healing begin.

*Dear God, when I pray for (not about) other people,
help me remember You want to change my perspective
on the toughest situations. Sometimes I don't feel like
praying for others because I don't want them to experience
forgiveness. I'm sorry for this selfish response. Forgive
them in the same way You've forgiven me. Amen.*

### CHALLENGE

Create an "impossible prayer" list. This should include
people you don't think will ever change, relationships
that will never be made right, and people who you
believe will never follow Jesus. Be transparent with God
and tell Him you think these requests are impossible.
Then acknowledge you serve the God of possible. Track
the results.

Have you ever refused to pray for someone because you
weren't sure you wanted them to experience forgiveness?
How does your prayer life change when you become
transparent with God about the struggles you have
with praying for others?

*Saturday—Evening*

Praying for others can be one of the hardest of God's
commands to follow. You can either think more about
*your* needs or find it unbearable to pray for people you
don't think deserve God's help. For the past seven days,
you've read many biblical reasons to pray for people
who've never once made it to your personal prayer list.
Take the challenge—add them.

> *Dear God, I think it's possible I will find other aspects
> of prayer more comforting. I think I'll be more willing to
> pray other personally acceptable prayers. Help me accept
> Your command to pray for people made in Your image,
> forgiven by Your Son, and loved beyond their sin. Amen.*

**CHALLENGE**

Track how your thinking is changing toward people
you're praying for during the next few months.

## REFLECTION

Make a list of the people you'd like to pray for. What names have been included in this list that weren't included last week?

How do you think praying for others could lead to less gossip?

*Week 2*

# PRAYING FOR MYSELF

*Unless the heart is right the prayer must be wrong.*
UNKNOWN

Self-help is a huge industry. From life-coaching to motivational seminars, books to podcasts, many are earning a living by doing their best to help others achieve personal goals. Self-help thinking has heavily influenced prayer.

In praying for others the pray-er may ask God to make their latest business venture successful. When you pray for yourself you may ask God for opportunities that will improve your finances, social standing, and personal life goals.

There was a time when praying for a tangible item beyond daily needs was a low-priority prayer. People believed that God had an agenda, and it made sense to align prayers with God's plan.

Coming to God with a list of *gimmes* seemed a very unfocused prayer with a laser-focused personal motive. Instead of learning the types of prayers God loves to hear, people sought to ask God to pay attention to what they wanted, give the item quickly, and remain available to positively fulfill their every wish.

This week you'll read scriptures that help put God's plan for personal prayer in perspective. While it's perfectly acceptable to pray for what you need, there are many essential things you never pray for. You'll be asked to be bold in your prayers, use your prayer time to dream big dreams, and to focus on your relationship with God and how to improve that relationship.

Prayers for yourself can help keep evil away, improve your spiritual vision, and order an on-time delivery of wisdom. Every time you pray for yourself you'll be inviting a close relationship with the God who isn't a puppet, rich uncle, or street magician.

He's not the God of parlor tricks. He's not bent on a social media following. He has a plan. He loves His people. He's in the job of changing lives. That includes yours.

Over the next seven days you'll learn that prayer is more than a divine concession stand. You'll discover that God actually wants you to pray for yourself. You'll discover the reasons why praying for yourself should not be ignored.

Praying for yourself is equal parts preparation, restoration, and consecration. It's establishing the course of your life and using God's resources to bring you to the crossroads of *God's Will Way* and *New Hope Drive*.

The reason to learn more about prayer is less about making a mistake and more about making the most of the time you spend talking with the God who not only has a plan for your future but wants to give you the wisdom to know how to follow His plan.

It's hard to engage in *self-help* when it conflicts with *God's help*. He knows what you need and can help you understand His plan for your life. Keep reading. Access to God's plan for your life is coming up. It shouldn't be a surprise that learning His plan starts with prayer.

# THE PRAYERS YOU PRAY

*"Ask."*
MATTHEW 7:7 NKJV

Do you have a need? Ask. Do you have a personal struggle? Ask. Do you want to know what your future holds? Ask.

God owns all the resources. He's the founder of compassion. He's the sustainer of all creation. He's the One you—ask.

Prayer is an opportunity. Tell God about the things that concern you. When fear threatens to overwhelm every part of your life, talk to the God who calms storms (Mark 4:35–41), is known as light (1 John 1:5), and offers comfort (2 Corinthians 1:3). If you believe what you're asking for is in your best interest—ask. Psalm 84:11 says, "For the LORD God is a sun and shield; the LORD will give grace and glory; no good thing will He withhold from those who walk uprightly" (NKJV). This is the God you ask. This is the God who gives you His best.

Children learn that if they never ask their parents, then they never give their parents the chance to say yes. In other words, if you never ask, the answer will always be no.

Prayer is a statement of dependence (John 15:5), a cry of desperation (Psalm 50:15), and the key that unlocks the desires of your heart (Psalm 37:4).

Start this week with this good news. God's for you. He always has been. His answers to your most personal prayers focus on a big picture only He can see. Walk with Him, and let Him show you the good things He has planned for you.

Pray and learn more about God as He responds to your every "ask."

## Sunday—Morning

God is not surprised when you feel insignificant. He understands both your reluctance to ask for what you need and your desire for something that's not good for you. He never condemns when you ask, but He reserves the right to give you what you need regardless of what you ask for.

*Dear God, I don't always know what to pray for. Sometimes I refuse to ask because I don't think I deserve Your help. May I always remember You want me to be honest with You. You want to hear words that reflect the core of who I am. Help me accept Your answer and learn from Your response. Amen.*

### Challenge

Write down three things that you've been afraid to ask God for. Think about each item and whether you think it's good for you and why you haven't asked before.

### Reflection

How will you be more honest with God in your next
    prayer time?
What stood out to you in today's reading?

## Sunday—Noon

Best friends are the people you turn to when you have a need. You've developed the language of relationship and you trust that you can depend on them. You can even impose if needed because you know their friendship is that close. Prayer is the step that leads to a similar relationship with God. The closeness of private prayer conversation will always reinforce trust in this most important friendship.

*Dear God, I want the closeness of a friend in my relationship with You. May my prayer life transform my willingness to trust You with the answers I need. May I be less interested in having You say yes and more interested in Your plans for my future. Amen.*

### CHALLENGE

Spend some time thinking of a prayer that you believe God will say yes to. Write this prayer request down, and explain why you think God would agree to the request.

### REFLECTION

What one prayer request are you grateful that God said no to?

Why do you think it's important to be willing to accept God's answer to your prayers?

## *Sunday—Evening*

Refusing to pray is like needing an answer but refusing to ask someone who knows. Refusing to pray is like needing help yet refusing to make a phone call. Refusing to pray can look a bit like pride because you may be telling God you don't value His help.

*Dear God, I am sorry when I treat prayer like a surface conversation. I settle for small talk when You want me to ask the deep questions that invite Your wisdom. I settle for the day's highlights and refuse to admit deep hurt. Help me to stop settling for being an acquaintance and remember You can be my closest friend. Amen.*

### CHALLENGE

You've listened to small talk. Think about whether this type of conversation reminds you of a close relationship or something less personal than real friendship. Write down some of the ways you can detect small talk and why it seems impersonal.

### REFLECTION

Since God is all-knowing (Psalm 147:5), why do you hesitate to ask Him questions only He can answer?

If you refuse to ask God for help, why are you surprised when you struggle?

*Week 2: Monday*

# DON'T HOLD BACK

*Let us draw near with confidence to the
throne of grace, so that we may receive
mercy and find grace to help in time of need.*
HEBREWS 4:16 NASB

As a child you likely knew that if you were in trouble you should talk to your parents. You didn't want to. You tried to figure things out on your own. In the end, you sadly explained your unfortunate situation.

In most cases, parents help children through tough circumstances. Parents may not be able to shield their children from all the consequences of poor decision making, but their love offers hope. Hope brings confidence. Confidence allows you to bring your problems to your parents sooner the next time around.

This is the picture of personal prayer. God is your Father. God has given you all the rights of a son or daughter (that's grace). God might even choose to withhold punishment (that's mercy).

Imagine being so free in your relationship with God that there is no hesitancy in prayer. You aren't a nuisance. You aren't interrupting. You don't bring anything to God that He won't be concerned about. You need someone to talk to—and He listens.

Even when you don't know exactly what to say, God understands. Prayer at its core is a white flag of surrender.

Prayer says, "I give up. I can't fix this on my own." Prayer invites God to merge your struggle with His answer. Prayer suggests a partnership between the God of answers and a child with questions.

Don't wait until you think you know how to pray, pray anyway. Then let your *God conversation* grow.

## Monday—Morning

God wants you to show respect, but that doesn't mean staying away from conversation with Him. He invites you to talk, welcomes your perspective, and longs to hear your concerns. Be polite, but come boldly. Be gentle, but share fully. Be respectful, but request the help you need.

*Dear God, may I always be reminded that my prayers are not a burden to You. Help me be confident in sharing my struggles. Help me be transparent in honestly telling You about the good, bad, and ugly parts of my human struggle. Thank You for the mercy and grace that meet me at every Dear God moment. Amen.*

### Challenge

Consider three things you struggle with but you've never asked God to help with. Consider three things in today's reading that might encourage you to ask for help for the first time.

Have you ever wanted to pray and thought you were
bothering God? Why did you feel this way?

Why should you quickly identify prayer as the best first
response?

*Monday—Noon*

Self-sufficiency is an honored concept in Western lore and
modern off-grid living. These rugged individuals work to
live without the aid of others. There is a sense of pride
that comes from relying only on yourself. There's danger
in trying to apply the same logic to your relationship with
God. Off-the-grid spiritual living is a recipe for destruc-
tion and setback.

> *Dear God, sometimes it's hard for me to believe You*
> *have the time to hear my concerns. I feel as if I should*
> *do everything I can to fix issues before I ask You for help.*
> *May I willingly pray to You about my concerns so there is*
> *nothing between us. Help me remember You are the God*
> *who makes possible what seems impossible. Amen.*

**CHALLENGE**

You struggle. You've tried to fix life on your own. Take
that struggle to God in prayer and admit you can't fix
it. Write down how easy or difficult it was to pray this
prayer.

Why do you think prayer is often a last resort rather than
a first response?
How is surrender to God a positive decision?

## Monday—Evening

Let's restate something found in today's reading. God's
love gives you hope. Hope instills confidence in the
Hope Giver. Confidence should encourage you to bring
problems to God sooner the next time around. Don't
picture God as one who punishes and then asks questions.
God wants you to ask questions so He can help you in
your time of need. His mercy and grace join you in prayer.

*Dear God, I want to experience the hope that makes me
confident enough to come to You the moment I'm in trouble.
I want the invitation of mercy and grace to meet me in
prayer and then be passed on to those I encounter. When I need
help I want to remember I should come to You first. Amen.*

### CHALLENGE

Instead of thinking of prayer as something you do in a
crisis, think of prayer as a way to learn God's mind about
your every concern.

### REFLECTION

How do you think a better prayer life could change the
way you think of God?
This evening you discovered what gives hope. What is it,
and how does it lead to an improved prayer life?

# A PRAYER OF AUDACITY

*Jabez prayed to the God of Israel: "Bless me, O bless me! Give me land, large tracts of land. And provide your personal protection—don't let evil hurt me." God gave him what he asked.*

1 Chronicles 4:10 MSG

This prayer seems out of place. The rest of the chapter is populated with verses listing the sons of Jewish family leaders, yet two verses are dedicated to the memory of Jabez. They provide great prayer instruction.

In verse 9 Jabez is described as "a better man than his brothers, a man of honor." This gives us a clue that when Jabez prayed this prayer his relationship with God was strong. His heart must have been well connected to the plan God had for him.

Verse 10 offers a prayer that some might think outrageous. Jabez asked God to bless him, give him lots of land, protect him, and keep him from evil. This is a prayer with roots in audacity. Jabez was fearless, bold, courageous, and confident. He must have known God could say no. He prayed anyway.

This prayer ends on the right note. Jabez asked for greater blessing but ended by asking God to keep evil away. If this part of the prayer was the only thing God would give Jabez, then God's protection of Jabez spared him from envy, greed, and covetousness. If God gave everything Jabez asked for, then protection from evil would keep him from pride, self-reliance, and independence from God.

God took a bold prayer with a right motive and gave Jabez what he asked for. He gave you an example.

## Tuesday—Morning

God speaks of blessings in terms of His ability to provide. This could be in the form of money and land, or it could be in relationships and meeting your daily needs. God knows wealth can create a relational problem between Himself and mankind. Because you are uniquely designed by God, He knows exactly what you need. He always gives what is best for you.

*Dear God, I want to be so close to You that I have some understanding of the big dream You have for my life. Once I understand Your plan, I can pray with audacity and boldness. I can ask for things that will help me do the job You created me to do. Amen.*

### CHALLENGE

Think of a need in your community that you identify with. If you're ready to pray a prayer of audacity, then ask God's help in fulfilling this need in ways only He can. Track the results.

### REFLECTION

If you could ask God to give you anything, what would it be?
Why do you think God should answer this prayer?
Why do you think God gave Jabez what he asked for?

*Tuesday—Noon*

The greater your relationship with God, the more treasured your prayer times. Friends are valued for their ability to listen. God should be valued for the same reason. No subject is off-limits. No concern is too small. No hope too big to express. Pray. Learn. Grow.

*Dear God, why is it so hard for me to pray the prayers
of a friend? I treat You formally and reverently,
but I stumble and feel disconnected from something that
should be meaningful. Help my prayers be filled with
respect, honesty, and a desire to know You better. Amen.*

## CHALLENGE

Think about prayer in terms of God's willingness to listen to everything that's important to you. Now think of reading God's Word as your willingness to listen to everything He has to say in response.

## REFLECTION

Why do you think the connection between prayer and reading the Bible is so strong?
Is prayer easy or hard for you? Why?

## *Tuesday—Evening*

Many Bible characters prayed that God would keep them from evil. More than a prayer based in superstition, these men and women understood that their relationship with God was altered when they became a disciple of evil. Because no one has the strength to handle upcoming struggles, ask God to keep evil away. Righteous living begins when you understand there really is a difference between doing whatever you want and honoring the God who provides the greatest defense against evil.

*Dear God, I'd like to say I am immune to the effects*
*of evil, but I'm not. I would like to say I don't need*
*Your help, but I do. I'd like to say I never sin, but I can't.*
*I have always needed Your help, and I need it today.*
*Keep me from evil: the kind I choose, the kind I*
*stumble into, and the kind I entertain. Amen.*

### CHALLENGE

Think about the last time you encountered evil. List two ways you believe the outcome could have been different if God's protection had been requested in prayer.

### REFLECTION

If you could avoid some of the effects of evil, how would that improve your spiritual life?
Does it seem wrong to pray that God would keep you from evil? Why?

# BROKEN AND TURNED AROUND

*Generous in love—God, give grace! Huge in mercy—
wipe out my bad record. Scrub away my guilt,
soak out my sins in your laundry.*
PSALM 51:1–2 MSG

King David was considered a man after God's heart, but his sinful nature also made him a guilty man. He suffered the consequences that came with sin's choice.

David's response is a great example. Before you pray for what you want, or name people you're praying for, you should be transparent with God about your spiritual life. If you sin, agree with God that what you did violated His law. Reacquaint yourself with a right relationship with God.

David remembered God's love, grace, and mercy and asked for a clean slate. He wanted his record expunged. He wanted God to repair his life damage. This wasn't a checklist prayer. This was the prayer of a broken man who'd broken God's law and wanted to break the cycle of sin.

Verse 3 says, "I know how bad I've been; my sins are staring me down." David understood that living with sin simply reminded him of a damaged friendship with God.

Verse 4 says, "You're the One I've violated, and you've seen it all." David is not trying to get away with his sin. He's trusting that the God of love knew the best remedy for a dark heart. David knew he hurt God, that God was witness to his sin, and that He was the final judge. Still, David prayed.

When you turn from sin, you're welcomed back into the arms of the One who calls you home.

## *Wednesday—Morning*

It can be easy to think that God's grace means you don't need to apologize when you sin. David's example shows that talking with God about sin (confessing) is part of His restoration plan. God wants you to admit your guilt, ask for His help, and turn toward obedience.

*Dear God, I don't want anything to come between us. I don't want to hide, live with regrets, or turn away from You. Help me accept the truth that telling You about my sin is the best way to turn toward You when I need You most. Amen.*

### Challenge

Consider one sin that's keeping you from being as close to God as you want. Consider who's hurt most by the separation.

### Reflection

How do you feel when you recognize you've sinned?
How do those feelings influence a close relationship with God?

## *Wednesday—Noon*

Being close to God is the best way to share your concerns, express your joys, and voice your sorrow. When there's something between you and God, these moments of sharing become clouded, ritualistic, and reduced to a spiritual checklist. When this becomes routine, prayer becomes less important because it's hard to remain close to someone you've offended without also agreeing you were wrong.

*Dear God, when I break Your law, help me remember to run to You. Help me admit I was wrong. Help me live with Your justice and rejoice in Your grace. When my back is turned because I am either embarrassed or defiant, please love me enough to break down the walls I put up and welcome me back to a restoring conversation. Amen.*

### CHALLENGE

Think about a time when you eagerly and immediately came to God to talk about your sin. Write about how you felt when you understood you were forgiven.

### REFLECTION

What stood out to you most in today's reading?
Why do you think it's important to talk to God about your sin before you pray for other people?

## *Wednesday—Evening*

God is never taken off guard when you admit you've sinned. He already knows what you've done. Like so many things in His Word, the reason we follow His rules is because His commands maintain and restore relationships. Sin separates us from God, but it also separates us from the people we sin against.

*Dear God, I don't want to forget that my sin not only stops me from being close to You, but it also keeps me from being close to the person I've offended. Help me learn that sorrow for breaking Your commands is the best step to improved relationships and restored understanding of Your Word. Amen.*

### CHALLENGE

Write down the name of someone you've offended. Think about ways you might be able to do the right thing in restoring a relationship with them. Choose at least one way you might be able to restore the relationship, and write down the benefits of restoration.

### REFLECTION

What one step can you take today that will bring you a step closer to God and a step closer to others in the aftermath of personal sin?

How does what you learn change the way you view prayer?

*Week 2: Thursday*

# A GIFT GOD WANTS

*Give all your worries and cares to God,*
*for he cares about you.*
1 PETER 5:7 NLT

Maybe you face control issues or a lack of trust, but the God who loves, forgives, and offers a forever life with Him asks for a gift you don't need—worry.

God wants everything that gives you ulcers, keeps you up at night, and insists you obsess over every worst-case scenario.

Fear and faith struggle to occupy the same space. For faith to grow, fear needs an eviction notice. Faith restores what fear destroys, puts out a welcome mat where a no trespassing sign had been posted, and invites trust to replace suspicion.

A gift ungiven is not really a gift. The gift has to move from your possession and ownership to someone else in order for a gift to be received.

God wants you to give Him complete ownership of every worry, concern, and fear you experience. He can handle it. He asks for it. He loves you.

God has no interest in allowing these troublemakers a ringside seat in your relationship with Him. When you allow fear and worry to become houseguests, it will affect relationships with everyone.

Because God doesn't worry, and because He knows

you do, He asks for your worries and cares. He knows you don't need them, have trouble dealing with them, and will waste time and energy that could be used in growing a relationship with Him.

Pray, and pass along a *worry gift* to the God who has everything. What you don't need He can replace with a transformed future.

## *Thursday—Morning*

It can be easy to miss the importance of today's verse. God doesn't just ask you to tell Him about your worries—He wants you to *give* Him the worry. He wants you to transfer ownership of every care and let Him deal with it. He has no interest in sharing ownership of your gift. When He owns your worry, you should stop trying to buy it back.

*Dear God, I've wasted time trying to keep a gift You want. Worry has been a go-to response for me. Today, I want to transfer ownership of something I've accepted as my responsibility. Help me understand what it looks like to give You all the things that make me anxious— and then trust You to take care of them. Amen.*

### CHALLENGE

When you have time, check out some of the other things God says about worry. Here are a few thoughts to get you started: Philippians 4:6–7; Matthew 6:25–34; Proverbs 12:25; Luke 12:25. Write down your thoughts.

Why do you think giving worry to God is such a hard
  gift to give?

Why do you think God wants your worry?

## Thursday—Noon

You might be afraid that God will not be able to handle
your fearful situation or that He might look down on you
because you were afraid. 1 John 4:18 says, "There is no
fear in love; but perfect love casts out fear, because fear
involves torment" (NKJV). God's love is a door showing
fear the way out of your life.

*Dear God, when I reject Your love in favor of fear, please
help me to rethink my decision. May I accept Your love so
You can accept my fear. Let me give You what I don't need
so I can accept the peace only You can give. You've proven
Yourself faithful every day of my life. Help me trust Your
faithfulness, accept Your love, and surrender my fear. Amen.*

### CHALLENGE

Make a two-column list. On one side, list the benefits of
worrying. On the other side, list the benefits of peace.

### REFLECTION

What do you worry about the most?

What would you have more time for if you didn't worry?

### Thursday—Evening

God doesn't worry. He doesn't need to. He knows the outcome of everything. He's not anxious when trouble visits His family. He offers grace for difficult moments, gives strength when weakness comes, and works all things together for good to those who love Him and are part of His family. He can accept your fear and worry because once He truly owns it, He makes it go away.

*Dear God, it's hard for me to believe You never worry. Fear is something that's far too easy for me to embrace. Sometimes the world seems out of control. Sometimes I think fear is the only way to respond. Help me trust that You know what You're doing and that You are working for my good. Amen.*

#### CHALLENGE

List your top five fears. Determine which fear will be your first gift to the God of *fear eviction*. Deliver that gift in prayer. Continue giving God more of your fear as your trust in Him improves.

#### REFLECTION

God is fully in control. How does this knowledge make it easier to trust Him?

What stood out to you in today's reading? How does it change things moving forward?

*Week 2: Friday*

# PRAYERS, MOTIVATIONALLY SPEAKING

*When you ask, you don't get it because your motives are all wrong—you want only what will give you pleasure.*
JAMES 4:3 NLT

You've learned that God wants you to ask Him for what you need. Today you'll discover the primary reason God might say no. God isn't a vending machine that dispenses what you want if you have enough spiritual change. He's not a genie that grants wishes if you happen to find Him in a giving mood. He's not a work boss that will allow you to barter promises for improved health, perfect family, job promotions, or something ranking in the top ten *shiny and new*. If God is all-powerful, then certainly He can get what you want. All you need to do is ask. Right?

Today's verse suggests that *motives* play a key role in how you pray and how God responds to your prayer. Fill your prayer with selfishness and ambition and you may find God replacing something you want with something you need. A new car might be replaced with patience. A job promotion might be set aside in favor of contentment. Health issues might lead to trust in the God who knows what you need more than you do.

God may be less concerned with your happiness than He is your willingness to accept His perfect gifts.

Happiness depends on circumstances. Circumstances rely on people who can disappoint. God doesn't disappoint. His gifts can always be received with joy, which never depends on circumstances.

## Friday—Morning

You wouldn't put a five-year-old on a roller coaster. You wouldn't give a peanut butter cookie to a person with a nut allergy. You wouldn't ask someone in a wheelchair to run a marathon. In each case you understand that even if they wanted these things it would not be in their best interest. God knows what's in your best interest, and if He says no or wait, there's a good reason.

*Dear God, motives play an important role in my life. Sometimes my motives are good and show that I want to help and be helped. Sometimes my motives are not so great and focus on what I want and how I'm going to get it. Help me pay attention to my motives when I ask for Your help. Amen.*

### CHALLENGE

Think of something you've wanted for a long time. Seek to identify the motive behind your desire.

### REFLECTION

How can you identify the difference in motives when praying?
Why do you think it's possible to overlook God's gifts when they seem so different from what you prayed for?

## Friday—Noon

God doesn't show preferential treatment among those who pray. It can seem that way when you believe God always says yes to the prayers of someone you know. Maybe this person has learned to pray for things God already wants to do. By learning what God loves, your prayers will change.

*Dear God, You want the best for me, but I can act as if You need help understanding my need. Remind me that I'm the one praying and You're the One who knows my life story. You can accomplish more when I accept what You wisely offer. Amen.*

### CHALLENGE

Prayers that come from a place of desperation can originate in humility, but they can also be spoken from a place of selfishness. Consider prayers that might be prayed under both circumstances. Note the differences.

### REFLECTION

Can you recall a time when you assumed that because you asked God for something He had to respond with a yes?

How do you think your motives and God's plan connect in the way God answers prayer?

## *Friday—Evening*

Circumstances can cause you to become happy or sad. Circumstances are not a good indicator of God's blessing. When you pray and God sends what He knows will be a blessing to you, don't be surprised if it arrives in the form of something unexpected. It might even seem the opposite of what you hoped for. Be encouraged. God's blessings inspire joy, which is always preferred to happiness and lasts much longer.

*Dear God, help me accept the joy You send with*
*Your gifts instead of settling for happiness with my*
*earned possessions. May I accept Your gifts even when*
*I don't understand them. Help me see that my motives*
*affect Your answer to my prayers. Amen.*

### CHALLENGE

Think about blessings you've received from God that didn't seem like blessings at the time. Think how this truth changes your view of prayer.

### REFLECTION

Why do you think it's possible to settle for things that bring happiness when joy is God's better gift?
How often do you equate positive circumstances to God's blessing? Is this always an accurate indicator?

# PRAY FOR THE WAY

*Show me the way I should go,*
*for to you I entrust my life.*
PSALM 143:8 NIV

Without a map, GPS, or written directions, getting to any destination is much harder. When you remove landmarks, stars, and road signs it's almost impossible to find places twice. God never intended to keep you in the dark about life's direction.

Jesus told His disciples He would send a Helper (John 14:26). God promised enough light to guide each next step (Psalm 119:105). He said that wisdom is a great pursuit (Psalm 90:12).

Wisdom is yours for the asking. When you pray for yourself, pray for wisdom to know how to pray. When you pray for yourself, ask for wisdom in understanding God's Word. When you pray for yourself, seek direction on dealing with relationships. If you need wisdom—ask.

So often prayers are filled with a list of *must have* items that don't impress God much. This week you've learned many things that God said you should pray for when it comes to what you really need. God doesn't want you to be uninformed, so pray for guidance. God doesn't want you to be a target for evil, so pray for protection. God doesn't want anything to get in the way of relationship, so confess sin when you pray. God doesn't want wrong motives to enter the conversation, so grow when you pray.

Prayer is a pass that gets you backstage at *God's wisdom event*. It offers valuable coaching sessions with the Holy Spirit. It brings light to dark questions, faith to trust issues, and joy to God's perfect answers.

## *Saturday—Morning*

Poor driving instructions can leave you frustrated. You might have to ask a second person for better directions. Sometimes people will contradict each other on how to get to where you're going. God provides clear directions, but He can't be held responsible if those instructions aren't followed. You need wisdom. He's got it. Pray.

*Dear God, You've given so many examples of people who've prayed for themselves. Help me pay attention to the types of prayers they prayed. I'm sorry for focusing more on what I want than on how I can be more like You. Amen.*

### CHALLENGE

Use an online search tool to find prayers in the Bible. Pick two. Find the common traits between these prayers.

### REFLECTION

What did you hope to learn when you started reading this book?
How has your view of prayer changed during these first two weeks?

## *Saturday—Noon*

The term *wisdom* is subjective. People can have many different definitions. Wisdom might be in how to make one's income spread further. Wisdom might be in wealth-making decisions. God's definition is simple, yet profound. God's wisdom is applying His truth and insight to your life so the plans He has for you become clear and achievable.

*Dear God, may I never settle for common sense
when I also need Your wisdom. Both are great gifts,
but they're not the same gift. Help me to allow Your
wisdom to change my thinking, challenge my choices,
and bring me closer to You. Amen.*

### CHALLENGE

Make a two-column list labeled "Common Sense" and "God's Wisdom." List things that are unique to each. Thank God for both, but spend time nurturing wisdom.

### REFLECTION

How do you think it's possible for someone to have common sense but no use for God?

In what ways are you blessed because you can ask for and receive God's wisdom?

*Saturday—Evening*

Praying for yourself is simply asking God to help you keep close to what deepens your relationship with Him, while keeping you away from those things that disrupt your growth. This week you've had the opportunity to see what this looks like and read examples of men who captured part of God's heart when it comes to prayer.

*Dear God, You love me with a forever love. You pursue me with the determination of One who knows I need rescue. You want me to learn and invite me to ask for Your wisdom. May I respond to Your love with a determination to seek Your truth, follow Your plan, and show no fear in asking You for direction. Amen.*

## CHALLENGE

Make three columns. Name them "Seek God's Truth," "Follow God's Plan," and "Ask God for Directions." In the individual columns, list three ways you think you can do each.

## REFLECTION

Why do you think God is quick to answer prayers for wisdom?

Why would you try to figure things out on your own when God invites you to request spiritual direction?

## Week 3

# PRAYING GOD'S WILL

*Don't pray to escape trouble. Don't pray to be comfortable in*
*your emotions. Pray to do the will of God in every situation.*
SAMUEL SHOEMAKER

God's will can seem mysterious and unknowable. If good
things happen you might conclude it was God's will, and
if bad things happen, you might think you didn't pray
right. But what if God's will is more about His plans and
less about yours?

God's will isn't as mysterious as you might think. The
Bible is filled with God's will for everyone. Start there.
God wants you to ask for wisdom in knowing His will, but
He also wants you to follow the directions He's already
given.

Praying God's will is an opportunity to dream big.
It's an exercise in faith. God doesn't always give you what
you want, but He'll always supply what you need. Become
more familiar with the heart of God and you can begin
to pray prayers He wants to say yes to. You can move the
focus from your wants to His plan.

In the next week you'll discover bold prayers and
amazing promises. You'll meet two men who wanted to
see their country return to God. You'll learn why trust
enhances prayer and a lack of faith might bring a "no"
response from God.

God's will is advanced when you cooperate. It asks

you to grow up, trust more, set aside your personal agenda, and acquaint yourself with the God you pray to.

God isn't cruel. He doesn't make you guess when it comes to His plan. He gives you enough of His plan to develop a taste for following in His footsteps. He offers enough answers to inspire trust. He shares enough of His heart to demonstrate His great love for you.

In the next few pages you'll learn not only how to *pray for* God's will but how to *pray* God's will. One asks a question while the other makes a statement. Both are important in developing a closeness in the conversation that started when you agreed you need God's help. When you accepted Jesus' spiritual rescue the conversation became two-way. You pray, and God speaks to you through the Bible and His Spirit.

Praying God's will ties the prayers you pray for others and the prayers you pray for yourself together and offers them to God to deal with in the best way possible. Praying God's will isn't about finding a way to make God do what you want. It is about finding a solution specifically developed by God Himself. Praying God's will is an opportunity to let God know you're listening and agree to follow His plan.

This is the equivalent of spiritual mentorship from the Creator of all. He can teach. He offers wisdom. He won't be stingy with His plan. The question you must answer is whether you will trust His *will* when it conflicts with your *want*.

# THE PLACE BETWEEN

*Don't copy the behavior and customs of this world,*
*but let God transform you into a new person by changing*
*the way you think. Then you will learn to know God's*
*will for you, which is good and pleasing and perfect.*
ROMANS 12:2 NLT

There are *do-it-yourselfers* who want to accomplish everything themselves, there are babies who can't do much on their own, and there are those who discover God has a plan to meet them between these extremes.

There may be plenty of reasons to be self-sufficient. There may be equally as many reasons to let someone take care of things for you. In prayer, God doesn't want you to take charge, but you're encouraged to join Him on a spiritual ride along. Your thinking should change and your actions should shift as He works to take the old you and make a new creation.

Why is this important? Those who seek God's will through prayer should start by rejecting the idea that they should copy and paste *society's standards for acceptability.* Christians should understand that *God's* plan is good, pleasing, and perfect.

When you decide to copy the behavior and customs of society, you resist God's desire to transform you into a new person: someone who resembles Him in character, conduct, and perspective.

Like a baby, accept God's help. Like a do-it-yourselfer, understand there's a plan to be followed. Like a mature Christian, cooperate with the Plan Maker and discover that wisdom always follows obedience.

## Sunday—Morning

Praying for God's will is more than praying for yourself, more than praying for others, and more than a vague feeling of doing the right thing. You are inviting God to bring His influence into every area of life. From the future of your children to the halls of justice. From your career to your finances. From godly choice to how God might choose to correct sin. Praying for God's will indicates you trust His plan more than planning your next step.

*Dear God, it feels like praying for Your will means things would be completely out of my control. I would need to change my opinion for Your plan. I would need to trust that Your plan is for my good. I would need to obey even when I don't understand. Help me accept what I can't figure out. Help me follow Your plan. Help me be a mirror to Your will. Amen.*

### CHALLENGE

Name three things you believe are God's will for your life. Think about how you determined they were His will.

What stood out to you most in today's reading?
Why do you think submitting to God's will is so important?

*Sunday—Noon*

Praying for God's will is a bit like ending a war. You wave a white flag of surrender and accept plans you weren't sure you wanted. If this is a war, it's one you initiated. God has always desired relationship. When you reject His will, a struggle begins (James 4:4). You can either be in conflict for the rest of your life or accept the most comprehensive *life plan* customized for your future.

*Dear God, I don't want to be at war with You. I don't want to reject Your will, but there can be fear in not knowing every part of Your plan. Remove the barriers that keep me from being completely sold on Your plan for me. Amen.*

## CHALLENGE

Make a list of five things that keep you from praying God's will. Read them through each day this week. Track the ones you would remove from this list by week's end.

## REFLECTION

How does war language change the way you view God's will?
Why do you think it is so hard to surrender?

*Sunday—Evening*

*Do-it-yourself* Christians can feel as though they play a role in their own salvation. *Baby Christians* can feel as though they have zero responsibility. *Christian maturity* invites do-it-yourselfers to trust more, and baby Christians to cooperate more with God's will for their lives. The struggle may be knowing that at one point you were each of these examples.

*Dear God, thanks for leading and for inviting me to follow. Help me release my grip on personal life planning so I can begin to see the path You've prepared for me. Help me walk in Your steps, obey when You say stop, and learn from our times together. Amen.*

## CHALLENGE

Make a three-column list and label the columns "Do-it-yourselfer," "Baby Christian," and "Christian Maturity." Write down any memories of how you responded during each phase of pursuing God's will.

## REFLECTION

Would you view yourself as a do-it-yourselfer Christian? How might this trait conflict with God's will?
How does the term "cooperate" link with the command to "obey"?

# PRAYERS OF THE ZEALOUS

*Believe me, friends, all I want for Israel is what's best*
*for Israel: salvation, nothing less. I want it with all*
*my heart and pray to God for it all the time.*
ROMANS 10:1 MSG

The apostle Paul was a zealous guy. A zealot describes an individual with incredible enthusiasm who is eager to share an opinion. That was Paul. Once he accepted God's will for his life he had a new center for his focused enthusiasm.

The apostle didn't pray *small* either. He wanted *everyone* in his country to embrace their best life by accepting God's rescue plan made available through Jesus. Paul didn't pray, "I hope some people come to Jesus" prayers. He didn't leave anyone out. Paul indicated that if he had his way everyone in Israel would experience life change through Jesus.

Jesus said in Matthew 11:28 (NIV), "Come to me, all you who are weary and burdened, and I will give you rest." That's what Paul wanted—and he was praying God's will.

Anytime you can pray something you know God already wants, you can be sure you're praying a good prayer.

Paul could have prayed for good health for everyone in Israel, but he chose to pray for salvation. It's possible Paul understood that health, money, and possessions meant little if the person you're praying for still needs rescue.

Yes, *pray* for the physical needs of others, *help* others but make sure praying that people will accept God's salvation is the prayer of a zealous heart in favor of God's will.

## Monday—Morning

Matthew 16:26 (NLT) says, "What do you benefit if you gain the whole world but lose your own soul? Is anything worth more than your soul?" Paul knew the answer to these questions and he prayed for the spiritual rescue of his entire country. It was the passionate prayer of a man who cared more about people than the things they owned.

*Dear God, help me be more concerned about people than things. Help me care enough to want to see them find You. Open my eyes to the spiritual needs of those I meet, and help me be courageous in pointing to Your answer when I see their need. Amen.*

### CHALLENGE

Make a list of five people who need Jesus. Pray for them this week. Add to the list whenever you think of someone new. Track how this alters your concern for others.

### REFLECTION

Why do you think it's God's will to pray for people who need Jesus?

How does today's reading reconnect prayer to relationship?

*Monday—Noon*

The apostle Paul was eager to share Jesus with others. He was enthusiastic about the new life he had in Christ. He was connected to the source of Good News, and he was a staff reporter. Paul knew his audience and understood their need. No wonder his prayer was applied to everyone.

*Dear God, the number of people I influence may be smaller than that of the apostle Paul, but my friends need You, too. Help me care enough about them to share the source of rescue, plan of salvation, and path to Your will. Draw me close to You so I can care more for others. Amen.*

**CHALLENGE**

Think about the times you've been closest to God. Write down three ways this closeness changed relationships with others in a positive way.

**REFLECTION**

Why do you think salvation is viewed by Paul as the primary need of his country?
What part of today's reading presents the greatest personal challenge?

## Monday—Evening

When the apostle Paul prayed for God's salvation to be real in the lives of everyone, it's possible the cynic in you thought, *It's just a lot easier to pray for "everyone" than to name names.* Paul's concern is evident in today's verse. He prayed for others, "all the time."

*Dear God, help me make prayer for the salvation of others a top prayer priority. I can't take things with me to heaven, but I meet people who need to know and love You. May my prayers offer introductions of lost people to the God who loves to find and be found. Amen.*

### CHALLENGE

Take one name on your morning prayer list and ask them one question: "How can I pray for you?" If this seems too hard, consider letting them know you're praying via note, text, e-mail, or social media messaging.

### REFLECTION

What do you think is the main reason God wants people to accept His rescue plan?

Can you think of ways you can take the importance of salvation and personally share that plan with others?

*Week 3: Tuesday*

# A PLACE OF FAITH

*When you ask, you must believe and not doubt,*
*because the one who doubts is like a wave of the sea,*
*blown and tossed by the wind. That person should*
*not expect to receive anything from the Lord.*
JAMES 1:6–7 NIV

*Praying* God's will requires *trusting* God's will. God is faithful and will always provide an answer, but there are times when a potential yes answer can be set aside due to a lack of faith.

If you were to pray for God's help, but believe He can't help, then help may not be coming. You have to be assured in your thinking that God is big enough to handle your prayer request.

It's one thing to admit to God that you struggle with trust, but another to mutter a monotonous prayer that has no personal conviction, direction, or trust in the outcome.

You must be convinced that God is big enough to handle your prayers even if He ultimately says no. Don't make conclusions about what God can and can't do. Trust. Don't doubt. His answer will be perfect.

James might easily have described a lack of faith in prayer as sloppy, directionless, and swayed by opinion. God *might* answer this kind of prayer, but James suggests you shouldn't count on it.

You could be guilty of praying, *"What can it hurt"*

prayers. These kinds of prayers are tossed up as *one among many* options when dealing with a personal crisis. These prayers don't come from a place of faith, but a mind willing to consider multiple solutions.

Pray, convinced that God can, and will, answer. Trust His decision.

## Tuesday—Morning

When you pray *one among many options* prayers it's easy to consider that if a crisis is averted there could be a reason *other than prayer* that contributed to life improvement. God said in Isaiah 42:8 (NIV), "I am the LORD; that is my name! I will not yield my glory to another." If you ask God for help and give someone else the credit, there is little reason for God to send help.

*Dear God, I want Your will, and I want to*
*trust Your ability to answer prayer. May I never be*
*thoughtless with my requests. May the words of my*
*mouth match the trust in my heart. May my mind*
*agree with Your Spirit. May Your answer bring quick*
*praise and gratitude from me to You. Amen.*

### CHALLENGE

Think of a time when you asked God for help but didn't believe He could or would. Recall His answer.

How often should you pray with full faith in God's ability to answer prayer?

Why do you think some people might pray even if they don't believe God will answer?

## Tuesday—Noon

God refuses to conform to any man-made standard. If you try putting God in a box of your own design you're indicating He only works in certain ways, at certain times, and with certain people. With so many cultures and languages around the world, God would be severely limited in what He could or couldn't do based on one person's experience. God sent a reminder in Isaiah 55:8 (MSG): "I don't think the way you think. The way you work isn't the way I work."

*Dear God, I want to remember that You are God and I'm just one among billions who need You. Help me remember You deal with me in a way that matches my need. You will deal with someone else in a different way. Such personal care is too awesome for me to truly appreciate, but thank You. Amen.*

**CHALLENGE**

Write down a few ways you can demonstrate faith in God's ability to answer your prayer.

Why do you think God might deal differently with each
individual?

Can you think of circumstances that have contributed to
your view of God? How has today's reading enhanced
or challenged that view?

*Tuesday—Evening*

Earlier you read that a lack of faith in prayer is "sloppy,
directionless, and swayed by opinion." A lack of faith cares
more about what other people think than what *the God
who made people* thinks. It trusts what it can see more than
what is unknown. It has a fickle opinion that can alter
with each new circumstance.

> *Dear God, I'm sorry for when I take a spiritual opinion
> poll. I regret thinking that You alter Your plans based on
> what people think. I am saddened when I think You could
> be as fickle as a human. Help me treat You with the
> honor that belongs to You. Amen.*

**CHALLENGE**

Make a two-column list labeled "God" and "Me." List at
least three things in each column that demonstrate the
differences you've discovered.

**REFLECTION**

Why should it be comforting that God isn't swayed by
personal opinion?

Why do you think God's answers are worth your trust?

# A MORE PERFECT DESIGN

*[May God] equip you with all you need for doing his will.*
*May he produce in you, through the power of Jesus Christ,*
*every good thing that is pleasing to him.*
HEBREWS 13:21 NLT

God's will should populate every area of your life. When you add prayer to your pursuit of God's will, you're assured that God provides everything you need to do what He asks.

James 1:17 says, "Every good and perfect gift is from above, coming down from the Father of the heavenly lights, who does not change like shifting shadows" (NIV).

Try drawing on your own strength and you'll miss opportunities to access God's great gifts. 2 Peter 1:3 says, "His divine power has given us everything we need for a godly life through our knowledge of him who called us by his own glory and goodness" (NIV).

When you accepted God's rescue plan through Jesus, you were given everything needed to understand the mystery of His grace (Ephesians 1:7–9), the perfection of His will (Ephesians 5:17), and thinking that transforms (1 Peter 1:13).

Like an architect, God has a blueprint for your life. Like an interior decorator, He has a design that is uniquely yours. Like an inventor, God has a purpose for your existence. But He's more than any of these. God didn't just create you to show off His skill. He created you because He loves you. He offers everything you need to be who He made you to be, because He sent His Son to restore your life. Ask God for what you need to follow His plan.

## *Wednesday—Morning*

Hebrews 13:21 is written in the form of a blessing. Those reading the words would understand that the writer wanted to be sure that the readers were connected to God's blessing. It included everything needed to do His will and to experience a life transformation that invited God to powerfully work in their lives. This was a blessing, a benediction, and a beautiful glimpse at a life that could be in the hands of a gift-giving God.

*Dear God, when I'm asking for Your help in knowing Your will, help me also pray You would do the same for others. May I be comfortable enough to ask for a blessing for others. May the words I speak, thoughts I think, and the concerns lodged deep in my soul match Your will for my life. Amen.*

### CHALLENGE

Consider your spouse, child, parent, or friend. Write a blessing for them based on Hebrews 13:21. Share it when appropriate.

### REFLECTION

How were you challenged in your thinking with respect

to seeing God's will as something you can know?
Why do you think God gives the gift of understanding
  when it comes to discovering His will?

## *Wednesday—Noon*

Today's reading featured many key verses related to God's
interest in making sure you can know His will. The reason
for listing these verses is a reminder that God's Word will
always be the best source for learning what God wants.
His Word unravels the mystery of following Him and is
the perfect resource for getting acquainted with His plan.

> *Dear God, help me know Your will and pray that Your
> plans will be accomplished. Help me cooperate in what
> You ask me to do, and help me share the good news
> that others can access Your plan for their lives. Amen.*

### CHALLENGE

Name two friends who are newer Christians. Make it a
priority to pray this week that they might know God's
will. If you're comfortable, share what you're learning
with them.

### REFLECTION

Why do you think there is such a strong connection
  between praying to God and reading the Bible?
What stood out to you in today's reading?

## Wednesday—Evening

A toaster is made to toast. A cell phone is made to communicate. Shoes are made to protect your feet. If you had no idea what any of these items were, you would have difficulty using them correctly. You would need someone to show you the purpose behind the product. God's will comes with instructions. When you can't figure it out, pray—then read His instructions.

> *Dear God, thank You for the kindness You show in sharing Your will for my life, giving me Your Word to explain Your plan, and for a passion to do the things You created me to do. Once I learn Your plan, help me be willing to cooperate with You. Amen.*

### CHALLENGE

Consider three reasons God's will is important to you. Write them down. Thank God for them.

### REFLECTION

Why do you think it would be cruel if God had a plan for your life but no willingness to share His plan? Why can you trust God's will for your future?

*Week 3: Thursday*

# THE OBEDIENCE FACTOR

*Teach me to do Your will, for You are my God;*
*let Your good Spirit lead me on level ground.*
PSALM 143:10 NASB

God wants you to become a student in His school of *divine life design.* Course requirements begin with gaining admission (you just need to ask in prayer) followed by tests and quizzes (graded by obedience to course requirements). You're never kicked out of the class (open-book tests are standard), but you may have to retake tests when you fail to follow instructions (prayer initiates a test restart).

In John 14:15 (NASB) Jesus said, "If you love Me, you will keep My commandments." In Luke 6:46 Jesus said, "Why do you call Me, 'Lord, Lord,' and do not do what I say?" James 1:22 says, "Prove yourselves doers of the word, and not merely hearers who delude themselves."

Reading the words isn't enough. God is interested in spiritual growth. Praying for God's will starts you on a great journey, but when you fail to obey what God's Word already says, you can't advance to a greater understanding of His will. Luke 16:10 (NASB) puts this in perspective: "He who is faithful in a very little thing is faithful also in much; and he who is unrighteous in a very little thing is unrighteous also in much."

If you want to know God's life plan for you, start with obeying what the Bible already asks you to do. Pray for help. Let God's Holy Spirit lead. Obey. If you want God to teach, be willing to learn. Start small. Be faithful. Grow.

## *Thursday—Morning*

Maybe it was simply a matter of observing human response. Certainly it was based on what God knew to be true. Man's faithfulness in small things is an indicator of how they would deal with big things. If you wait for God to give you big things before you show faithfulness to His plan, then your life may be remembered for the *waiting*.

*Dear God, thank You for pointing out ways I can stop putting my life on hold. Help me become faithful in reading Your instructions. Help me be trustworthy in doing what You ask. Help me to stop waiting for a big assignment when You've already given me something else to do. Amen.*

### CHALLENGE

Read Philippians 4:4–7. List some of the things God asks of you in these verses. Consider this an opportunity to be faithful in following one part of God's will for your life.

### REFLECTION

What is something you know God wants you to do that you don't want to do?

Why do you think it makes sense for God to share His will more fully with those who obey?

## Thursday—Noon

God gives you examples of His will and asks you to comply with His plan. Skipping over assignments seems easy enough, but the result is a lack of vision, a season of frustration, and believing God's will is always just out of reach.

*Dear God, keep me from dismissing parts of Your will that just don't seem convenient. Keep me from thinking I can excuse sections of Your will that I don't think should apply to me. Keep me from thinking Your rules are just for other people. Since I want to know Your will, help me follow what You've already told me. Amen.*

### CHALLENGE

Read 1 John 5:14–15 and think about how confidence in God's will leads to greater communication with God.

### REFLECTION

How can confidence in God's will develop the trust needed to obey?

How can obedience to God develop confidence in God's will?

## Thursday—Evening

Employees are given more responsibility when they show they can manage existing tasks. Children gain trust when they obey their parents. The plans God has for you will begin to make sense when you complete God's current assignments.

*Dear God, I want to be responsible. Help me be trustworthy. I want to believe in Your plan for me. Grow my faith. I want to make sense of Your plan. Give me wisdom. Amen.*

### CHALLENGE

Recall a classroom setting from your past. Think about the students who gained the teacher's trust. Consider reasons why that might have occurred.

### REFLECTION

How do you think God can help you obey His rules? Growing in faith is important. What steps can you take today to mature in your faith?

# GOD'S WILL—GOD'S WORD

*Be filled with the Spirit, speaking to one another
in psalms and hymns and spiritual songs, singing
and making melody in your heart to the Lord.*
Ephesians 5:18–19 nkjv

If you really want to ensure people know you're paying
attention to them, just repeat or rephrase what you
learned from what they said. If you're wrong, they can
correct you. If you're right, they'll be more interested in
communicating because you actually listened.

This is the idea behind praying God's Word back
to God. Try praying instruction from the apostle Paul's
letters or epistles. Repeat praise from the Psalms. Recount
the lessons Jesus taught.

If God's will hinges on God giving you answers
through His Word, then you deepen the connection to
His plan by repeating back to God (and to others) what
you're learning. Ask Him to help you understand what
you need to know about each passage you pray back
to Him.

This idea serves a dual purpose. It can encourage your
prayer life and it can motivate you to read more of God's
will through God's words.

God says in Isaiah 55:11, "So shall My word be that
goes forth from My mouth; it shall not return to Me void,
but it shall accomplish what I please, and it shall prosper

in the thing for which I sent it" (NKJV).

If you have trouble sharing your faith with others, then share His Word, "speaking to one another in psalms and hymns and spiritual songs." When you do, you encourage those who believe, challenge those who don't, and trust that God is doing what only He can.

*Friday—Morning*

If you've ever wondered how powerful God's Word is, consider Hebrews 4:12: "The word of God is living and powerful, and sharper than any two-edged sword, piercing even to the division of soul and spirit, and of joints and marrow, and is a discerner of the thoughts and intents of the heart" (NKJV).

> *Dear God, effective communication is important to me. I want to understand other people, and I want them to understand me. Help me listen to others in a way that shows I care. Help me listen to You in a way that shows I'm interested in what You have to say and how Your plans change my life. Amen.*

**CHALLENGE**

Think of someone who really listened to you. Think about how important that was to you, then try *really* listening to God by reading His Word.

Why do you think there is a strong connection between
  reading God's Word and understanding God's will?
How can you make praying God's Word a part of your
  prayer life?

*Friday—Noon*

If you've ever wondered if the Bible is filled with errors,
consider Luke 1:37: "The word of God will never fail"
(NLT). When you pray God's Word, you utter a perfect
prayer. It is the kind of prayer that shows God you're
listening.

> *Dear God, may Your words spoken by me bridge a*
> *connection between my mind and heart. May those*
> *words that hold meaning for You transform how*
> *I think. May Your words be something more than*
> *just another idea to consider. Amen.*

**CHALLENGE**

Consider the stages of your life and how the Bible factored
into those stages. Think about whether more time in the
Bible led to a greater connection to God. Write your
conclusion and review your answer when you struggle.

**REFLECTION**

Why do you think it's important to trust God's Word?
What stood out to you most in today's reading?

## Friday—Evening

If you've ever wondered how helpful God's Word can be, consider 2 Timothy 3:16–17, "All Scripture is given by inspiration of God, and is profitable for doctrine, for reproof, for correction, for instruction in righteousness, that the man of God may be complete, thoroughly equipped for every good work" (NKJV). If you want to learn, God's Word has always been the right book.

*Dear God, because Your Word is the primary way You speak to me, keep me from thinking only parts of the Bible are right. This belief can cause me to doubt everything You say. If I can't trust everything in Your Word, then what is truth? You gave the entire Bible to me as a book of instruction. Help me learn from You and believe that what I learn is truth. Amen.*

### CHALLENGE

If you have considered that parts of the Bible aren't true, then think for a while about what that means logically for your faith. Write down the struggles you might have with believing everything in the Bible. Then keep reading God's Word for answers.

### REFLECTION

Name four things 2 Timothy 3:16–17 says are profitable reasons to learn from the Bible.

Name a positive experience during a time when you both prayed and read God's Word.

# GOD'S WILL: ALWAYS IN SEASON

*[Josiah] did what was pleasing in the Lord's sight. . . .*
*He did not turn away from doing what was right.*
2 KINGS 22:2 NLT

In a time when everyone did what was right in their own eyes (Judges 17:6), an eight-year-old boy became king of Judah. He was different from previous kings. He believed God could be trusted. He believed God had a plan. He believed he was placed in a position of leadership to help reintroduce the people to their abandoned God.

The people had little communication with God because His Word had literally been hidden in the temple. No one had read the scriptures in a very long time. When God's will was uncovered and read, the young king was broken. He recognized the people weren't following God's will. They didn't have the information they needed. Josiah would become their example.

God could communicate through His Word, and the people feared hearing more than they wanted. Josiah instructed that everything God had written be read aloud to the entire nation. 2 Kings 23:3 says Josiah "pledged to obey the Lord by keeping all his commands, laws, and decrees with all his heart and soul" (NLT). The people followed their king's example and God was brought back into conversation with those who hadn't recognized His voice.

One of the greatest parts to God's will is conversation. He wants you to know what's important to Him so your decisions are informed by His desire. Then, if you choose to reject His will, it's because you made a choice, not because God didn't share His heart.

## Saturday—Morning

When you follow God's will, your example might encourage others to do the same. When you read God's Word you discover His heart. When you pray the prayer of the informed, God's plan includes your understanding.

*Dear God, I don't want to be uninformed. When it seems hard to read Your words, help me remember You are sharing Your heart. I can learn from You. I can follow You. I can help others do the same because even that is part of Your will. Amen.*

### CHALLENGE

Think of a time when someone who had a close relationship with Jesus influenced your decision to follow God toward deeper conversation and trust. Write down what was so influential about this person. Consider what you learned from their example.

### REFLECTION

What do you look for in Christian friendships?
What have you learned today that can help you identify those individuals?

*Saturday—Noon*

Age has little to do with your ability to follow God. Josiah began a nation-changing campaign when he was eight. Timothy was a young man the apostle Paul trained to lead people. Young people are not excluded from God's plan. Paul told Timothy, "Don't let anyone think less of you because you are young. Be an example to all believers in what you say, in the way you live, in your love, your faith, and your purity" (1 Timothy 4:12 NLT). Be encouraged. Follow.

*Dear God, never let my age be an excuse for not following Your will. Let me never say I'm too young to learn or too old to care. May every day be an adventure in discovering the better plan You have for me. May I arrive at the destinations You choose for me. May Your wisdom guide me. May my obedience allow You to transform this heart into Your character. Amen.*

## CHALLENGE

Think of individuals who are both older and younger that you admire for their walk with God. Identify ways their lives have encouraged you.

## REFLECTION

In what ways have you grown in your walk with Jesus over the last twelve months?
In what ways would you like to see growth in the next twelve months?

## Saturday—Evening

What you learn from God requires you to make a decision. If you say you love God but have hatred toward others, then you've made a decision that's out of character with God's will. If you accept forgiveness without forgiving, then you have a faith that is self-centered. You will make decisions every day. Those decisions either move you closer to God's will or further away.

*Dear God, may a decision to follow You be as dramatic as Josiah's decision to transform his culture through obedience. Help me allow You to do the work in my life that transforms and redirects my thoughts, actions, and attitudes. Amen.*

### CHALLENGE

Think of three recent life decisions. Write down what role God played in each choice.

### REFLECTION

What one decision you make today will you pray about first?
What characteristics of Josiah would you like to adopt?

*Week 4*

# PRAYING THROUGH
# TOUGH TIMES

*Only a life of prayer and meditation will*
*render a vessel ready for the Master's use.*
GEORGE MUELLER

When someone says, "How are you doing?" there is really only one answer most people find acceptable: "Fine." Those four words should indicate caring concern but have been redefined as a simple form of greeting. The question is not supposed to be answered with, "Well, until recently I was OK, but I messed up my shoulder and it's really made things difficult. Do you think you could help me move my china hutch?"

If this is your response, you can expect a confused look. You can also expect the person to stop asking "How are you doing?" They aren't sure they want to know.

Does this seem like a strange opening to a section on praying through tough times? It does provide a contrast between typical human response and the incredible response of a God who never wants you to walk through struggles alone.

God really does want to know how you're doing. He invites you to tell Him through prayer. He doesn't mind if you go into incredible detail. He doesn't need you to whitewash the pain, sugarcoat the description, or gloss over your response. God wants your honest account of difficult days.

This isn't so He can gauge the response of a test subject, it's not for statistical analysis, and it's not part of a psychological profile. He wants to know because He cares. He wants to know your heart because He can do something to help in stressful situations.

There are many reasons for struggles and you'll read more about them every day this week, but there's one common outcome for the struggles you face. If you pray, you will be more deeply connected with God, your faith will grow stronger, and your compassion for others will deepen.

You'll read about a king who murdered, committed adultery, and lived to develop a very close relationship with God. You'll learn about a prophet whose hard time arrived because he didn't want what God wanted. You'll read about a queen who faced death to save her people.

God doesn't require small talk. He doesn't need a warm-up monologue. He understands that in the middle of your struggles you'd rather be home with Him. Romans 8:23 says, "We believers also groan, even though we have the Holy Spirit within us as a foretaste of future glory, for we long for our bodies to be released from sin and suffering. We, too, wait with eager hope for the day when God will give us our full rights as his adopted children, including the new bodies he has promised us" (NLT).

While you're alive on earth there will be trouble (John 16:33). It just makes sense to understand how you should relate to struggle when it can't be avoided. This is the goal, purpose, and practicality of the next seven days.

*Week 4: Sunday*

# GET HERE SOON

*Be kind to me, GOD—I'm in deep, deep trouble again.
I've cried my eyes out; I feel hollow inside. My life leaks
away, groan by groan; my years fade out in sighs. My
troubles have worn me out, turned my bones to powder.*
PSALM 31:9–10 MSG

The pressures of life can wear you down. If they do, you can probably identify with this part of the psalmist's prayer. Ask God for kindness. Share how you feel. Share what you believe to be the outcome of your present crisis. Ask God for help. Plead for His mercy. Weep if you need to. Then, by trusting in God's help, refuse to stay in this dark place any longer.

If you only read the verses above you might think a pity-party prayer is the logical emphasis of your conversation with God. While you can pray this kind of prayer, you might be missing out on demonstrating trust that God is in control and can take care of your present pain. You aren't a bad Christian if you tell God about your honest struggle. You're not automatically a good Christian by refusing to invite God to your personal battles.

Later in Psalm 31 there is a tone that is a stark contrast from what you read above. Psalm 31:23–24 says, "Love GOD, all you saints; GOD takes care of all who stay close to him, but he pays back in full those arrogant enough to go it alone. Be brave. Be strong. Don't give up. Expect GOD to get here soon" (MSG).

You've shared your heart—accept His answer. Rejoice (Psalm 30:11).

*Sunday—Morning*

You will not find the phrase "God helps those who help themselves" in scripture. Psalm 31:23–24 seems to point to a completely different truth, "GOD takes care of all who stay close to him, but he pays back in full those arrogant enough to go it alone" (MSG). Going forward without God means you're arrogant enough to believe you're a better guide than God. You may be heading in a specific direction, but it's your plan—not God's. Only one plan never fails.

*Dear God, may I never get ahead of You, believing I know where I'm going. I don't want to fall behind and get lost. Help me walk by Your side and leave pride behind. When You lead me, help me keep my focus on each step into the future You've planned for me. Amen.*

**CHALLENGE**

Spend some time thinking about the last time you really struggled through a day. Write about how long it took from the moment you recognized it was a bad day until you took the day's problems to God in prayer.

**REFLECTION**

How has Psalm 31:23–24 challenged your thinking

when it comes to deciding how soon you come to
God with your bad day?

How might you be comforted knowing that everyone
struggles through difficulties?

*Sunday—Noon*

Perhaps the psalmist's words connected with your heart
when he said, "I've cried my eyes out; I feel hollow inside.
My life leaks away, groan by groan; my years fade out
in sighs" (Psalm 31:9 MSG). You've had moments when
you've evicted tears, tried to fill the empty space inside,
and felt as though you've wasted time. Your trouble doesn't
take God by surprise, and He's the only One who can fill
the emptiness within.

> *Dear God, when difficult days come, I'm grateful I can
> come to You with every groan, sigh, and tear. You're
> acquainted with grief and understand the frustrations
> that bring me to You broken. Thank You for Your
> willingness to bring comfort when I'm miserable. Amen.*

### CHALLENGE

List at least one way you can envision how coming to
God on the bad days could be personally freeing.

### REFLECTION

Have you ever felt condemnation when you come to
God broken? God doesn't condemn those in Christ
Jesus (Romans 8:1), so who do you think is doing the
condemning?

How does today's reading encourage you in an
  unexpected way?

*Sunday—Evening*

Today's reading described the use of a *pity-party prayer*.
The reason to avoid feeling sorry for yourself is that you
may begin to view yourself as a victim trapped in un-
controllable circumstances with people you dislike. Praying to God with transparency is one thing, but praying
in *pity-party mode* will leave your conversation with God
one-sided.

> *Dear God, You love me enough to intervene.*
> *You either change my circumstances or You change me.*
> *Help me avoid pity-party prayers. I am not a victim.*
> *I am Your child; loved, accepted, and forgiven. I don't*
> *need Your pity—I need Your help. Amen.*

### CHALLENGE

Write a pity-party prayer with all the things you find
annoying in your circumstances, the people who've hurt
you, and list why it seems unfair. Think about why this
may not be the best approach to prayer.

### REFLECTION

Why do you think a pity-party prayer might be selfish?
How can you be transparent in your prayers without
  hosting a pity party?

# STRUGGLE ENDURANCE

*Three different times I begged the Lord to take it away.
Each time he said, "My grace is all you need. My power
works best in weakness." So now I am glad to boast about
my weaknesses, so that the power of Christ can work through
me. That's why I take pleasure in my weaknesses, and in the
insults, hardships, persecutions, and troubles that I suffer
for Christ. For when I am weak, then I am strong.*
2 CORINTHIANS 12:8–10 NLT

There's a hard truth in today's verses; sometimes you won't
be relieved of a personal struggle. Your prayers will draw
you close to God, and He'll provide the grace you need.
The struggle might bring you clarity. The distress you
encounter could be to give you a front-row seat to God's
power when you give up *circumstance control*.

There will be times that a struggle will exist in spite of
your most passionate prayer. The struggle could produce
a crop of *organic endurance*. Romans 5:3–4 says, "We can
rejoice, too, when we run into problems and trials, for we
know that they help us develop endurance. And endurance
develops strength of character, and character strengthens
our confident hope of salvation" (NLT).

God won't always say yes to removing struggle
from your life. Sometimes the depth of struggle runs
parallel with the Christlike character God's forming
in you. Remember, the struggles you face aren't always
a punishment. Sometimes it's just a new mission in the

army of God. You could come through the battle wiser, more compassionate, and of greater use to God.

*Monday—Morning*

The "struggle is real" is a statement that's become cliché, but real struggles are an everyday visitor to humanity. It's possible to minimize their impact or project the idea that people who have real struggles just don't have all life's pieces put in place. Everyone struggles. Sometimes the struggle leaves a person breathless and frustrated. Maybe that's you. Maybe that's now.

> *Dear God, help me never minimize the struggles others face or dismiss the struggles I go through. Help me reach out to You even in those moments when it seems relief isn't coming, for Your comfort is offered in the struggle. Help me trust even when I don't understand. Amen.*

**CHALLENGE**

Have you ever felt like the apostle Paul, wondering why a struggle you've prayed about never seems to go away? Write down some of the things you went through in trying to understand.

**REFLECTION**

In what ways can you identify with the apostle Paul when it comes to struggles?

Can you name one thing you became grateful for
following a prolonged personal struggle?

*Monday—Noon*

If you run a race, endurance is the payoff for repeatedly
placing one foot in front of the other. Facing a battle with
God at your side offers protection even when the battle
continues. It offers companionship when others have
abandoned the effort, and it makes room for God to work
in the circumstances that would otherwise defeat you.

*Dear God, the toughest days of my life are made easier
knowing You love me. My darkest trials are illuminated by
Your presence. My longest nights are made easier knowing
You have my future secured. I'm grateful. Amen.*

### CHALLENGE

In those moments when you've felt as if you were alone,
God was with you. Consider how desperate things
would have been if God had not walked with you. Write
down your thoughts, express gratitude to God, and then
share what you've learned with someone you believe is
"walking alone."

### REFLECTION

How important is the concept of endurance when it
comes to praying through your battle?
How do you handle doubt when it comes to long-term
struggles?

## Monday—Evening

Earlier you read that sometimes the depth of struggle runs parallel with the Christlike character God wants for you. Perhaps your struggle is not only for your benefit but for the words of encouragement you'll be able to pass on to others in their struggle. God's will not only takes into account your needs but the needs of others.

*Dear God, Job struggled to understand Your will.*
*He wrestled with justice and righteousness, just like me.*
*My vision can get cloudy when I try to understand why I*
*struggle when it seems other people don't. Help me accept*
*what I need from You. Give me the grace to endure today.*
*Please send the same gift in the morning. Amen.*

### CHALLENGE

Think about God's grace and mercy. Write down ways you've seen both in your personal battles.

### REFLECTION

Do you have to understand everything about how God works in order to trust Him? Why or why not?

How can you see God using your story to help others?

# A "MORE THAN PRAYER" PRAYER

*"Go, gather together all the Jews who are in Susa,*
*and fast for me. Do not eat or drink for three days,*
*night or day. I and my attendants will fast as you do.*
*When this is done, I will go to the king, even though*
*it is against the law. And if I perish, I perish."*
ESTHER 4:16 NIV

Queen Esther was told her entire race was to be anni-hilated. Her husband, the king, was not aware she was Jewish when he signed the killing law. If you think the queen had the ability to just walk into the throne room and tell her husband there had been a mix-up, you'd be wrong.

One way Esther could visit the king was if he com-manded her to appear. The only other way was to show up unannounced. If the king held out his scepter, everything would be fine, but if he wasn't in the mood to see his wife, she could be put to death.

There was so much unknown to Esther, so much inner conflict, so much riding on her meeting with the king. Her *bad times* prayer invited every other Jew in Susa to pray for the success of the meeting. Esther understood that if there was to be a positive outcome, God needed to be involved.

The queen asked her people for one more thing: a fast. She wanted the people to have clarity in their prayers.

By asking for a fast she was saying this prayer was more important than food, comfort, and convenience.

Such prayerful dedication is the right choice.

## *Tuesday—Morning*

A fast is typically thought of as a time set aside where you don't eat so you can spend that time determining God's will for your life. In biblical times, giving up food was typically thought of as the primary sacrifice, but as other things have become important in culture, some people look to the possibility of an electronic fast. This could mean no TV, phone, or Internet. The idea behind a fast is to remove distractions from hearing God's voice (more on this next week).

*Dear God, give me a heart that wants what You want.*
*Give me a will that consults You whenever I need to*
*make plans. Give me a body that's willing to be deprived*
*for a time in order to understand Your voice. Amen.*

### CHALLENGE

Consider what's important to you. Write down one thing you could set aside today so you could learn more from God about how to handle what's most important.

### REFLECTION

What do you think would be a benefit to fasting? Why do you think it would be difficult to fast?

*Tuesday—Noon*

Struggles. They could come in the form of a call that informs you of an accident or could be unexpected, negative health news. You've likely experienced bad news that leaves you stressed out and anxious. When prayers just don't seem enough, you might try Esther's example. Fast and invite others to join you so you might hear God's answer to your predicament.

*Dear God, You made each human for relationship. Asking other people to pray may seem especially difficult when relationships are hard. Help me see that when people join together in prayer and fasting there is greater understanding of what You want and how to move forward. Help me be brave enough to enlist Your help. Amen.*

#### CHALLENGE

Name two people you believe you could count on to pray for you when trouble comes. Commit to asking them when struggles visit.

#### REFLECTION

What stops you from asking other people to pray for you?
How willing are you to pray for the struggles of others?

## *Tuesday—Evening*

Esther's request for prayer and fasting resulted in the salvation of her people (Esther 8). When people take God seriously, join each other in prayer for His will, and commit to setting aside what's comfortable to gain perspective, there's a spiritual shift for those involved (Ecclesiastes 4:9–10).

*Dear God, Your Word says that two are better than one. When I feel like I'm alone, remind me of Your presence. Remind me of those who follow You and are walking the same way with me. Help me trust You. Help me accept the support of others who trust You. Amen.*

### CHALLENGE

Think about the prayer of Esther. The help she enlisted should remind you of church. Take the time to write down the ways it does. Write down the ways it appears to be different.

### REFLECTION

What will you remember from today's reading that encourages relationships?

If you knew someone would pray with you, what would prevent you from asking them?

# NO TROUBLE-FREE ASSURANCE CLAUSE

*Even though I walk through the valley of the
shadow of death, I fear no evil, for You are with me;
Your rod and Your staff, they comfort me.*
PSALM 23:4 NASB

God never offered a life existence policy with a trouble-free assurance clause. However, God does offer roadside assistance every step of your life journey. He travels with you, prepares the way, and guides you through the toughest stretches of your spiritual Death Valley. If that doesn't instill confidence, consider Psalm 9:10: "Those who know Your name will put their trust in You, for You, O LORD, have not forsaken those who seek You" (NASB).

While God made this world perfect, the sin of Adam brought trouble to the family of man. God is with you every second, minute, hour, day, week, month, and year. He doesn't take holidays. He never calls in sick. Your prayers never go to voice mail. He always has time for you.

Prayer is an invitation for God to keep walking with you as you approach the rim of each mountaintop heading into a valley seemingly filled with evil, fear, and potential abandonment. God is the Master of all, and He's not intimidated by your Death Valley fears.

Hebrews 10:35 says, "Therefore, do not throw away

your confidence, which has a great reward" (NASB). You could be totally in the dark about your future, or even the next phase, but when God's got your hand, you can be confident with every step. On the other hand, take that walk alone and learn why "the valley of the shadow of death" is such an appropriate name.

## Wednesday—Morning

One of the greatest fears known to man is being left alone. Even the most meaningful relationship can't replace knowing, loving, and relating to God. Where others might abandon you, God never does. Where others might let you down, God helps you up. And when you have to walk through the darkest times, God brings His light and walks each step with you.

*Dear God, I don't want to be alone and I hate feeling lonely. Thanks for being close enough that I can talk to You whenever I need to. Thanks for lifting me up when I think I'm down for the count. Thanks for giving Your friendship when I was less than friendly. Thank You—for everything. Amen.*

### CHALLENGE

Turning to God in life's hardest moments is a wise decision. Consider whether it's been your first response in a crisis.

## REFLECTIONS

Do hard times make you feel more, or less, lonely? Why?
Who is the only one you can always count on in a crisis?

## *Wednesday—Noon*

Face trouble and you might call on God for help, but when
you're on a spiritual mountaintop it's easy to think you've
arrived spiritually and can probably handle some adversity
on your own. Maybe you can spare God some effort by
facing the dark road ahead alone. He wants to join you in
the journey. You need His companionship.

*Dear God, help me realize that when I try not to bother
You I am putting myself at jeopardy. When I walk alone
I am refusing Your protection, resisting Your help, and
rejecting Your companionship. I don't know why I do that.
Please, show my next step forward. Amen.*

## CHALLENGE

The next time you struggle, try changing your first
response. Instead of thinking about what you can do to
solve the issue, try asking God for help through the issue.

## REFLECTION

What stood out to you most in today's reading?
What are some of the reasons you don't ask God for help?

## *Wednesday—Evening*

You might be experiencing your own spiritual Death Valley right now. That may be the reason you found your way to this book. God's offer of help in this moment is no accident. It's not an offer to be taken away after a trial period. It's the personal assistance of God.

> *Dear God, give me the courage to face each struggle knowing You can be trusted. You're completely up-to-date on the circumstances I face. Help me remember You supply enough grace, share enough comfort, and give enough mercy whenever it's in my best interest. Amen.*

### CHALLENGE

Consider your best friendships. Write down reasons you might see those types of friendships improve when struggles come.

### REFLECTION

By human standards, how did God's work get harder when Adam sinned?

Why do you think it's important to God that you ask Him to walk with you in life's battles?

*Week 4: Thursday*

# THE BROKEN LIVES OF KINGS

*God, make a fresh start in me, shape a Genesis week
from the chaos of my life. Don't throw me out with
the trash, or fail to breathe holiness in me. Bring me
back from gray exile, put a fresh wind in my sails!*
PSALM 51:9–11 MSG

King David had reason to expect rejection from God.
He committed adultery when he knew God said it was
a sin (Exodus 20:14). He was deceitful about the event
(Jeremiah 17:9). He schemed to murder the woman's
husband (Exodus 20:13).

David committed crimes against God's law that he
wouldn't have tolerated in anyone else. It took a visit from
the prophet Nathan (2 Samuel 12) for David to realize the
incredible struggle he faced. From the pride of thinking
himself above the Law to one who humbly owned his sin,
the king turned to God for rescue. He asked for mercy
when the true penalty was death. He asked for restoration when he deserved a fractured future. He asked for
holiness while his life bore the stench of sin.

God could have said no to every one of his requests.
David did not have a right to forgiveness, but forgiveness has no substitute. Against every expectation, God
took this very bad time in the life of a king and remade a
future from the chaos of sin's choice.

When you sin, ask for forgiveness, turn away from the

*desperation path*, retrace your steps, and follow God once more. Don't hide yourself from the God who's restored the broken lives of kings.

## *Thursday—Morning*

You will sin. Everyone does (Romans 3:23). The easy choice is to believe that when you let God down He is no longer interested in a friendship with you. You can wallow in a pity that suggests you would rather die alone in your sin-choice than to face God who's described as being rich in mercy and whose love offers forgiveness (Ephesians 2:4–5).

*Dear God, the only place where I can find restoration is in Your presence. The only love strong enough to completely forgive is Yours. The only mercy that believes in my future is Yours. May I pursue what You offer me in my brokenness. May I refuse to run, and resist hiding. Amen.*

### Challenge

Using what you've learned so far, commit to pray that God will offer mercy, love, and forgiveness to someone you don't believe deserves it.

### Reflection

Why does it seem easier to hide from God than to confess sin?

What did you learn that makes you believe running to God is the best option?

## *Thursday—Noon*

It can be easy to look at the sins of others and find yourself standing with God by saying what they did was wrong. Sometimes Christians are less ruthless in identifying the sin in their own lives. God dealt with this issue in Matthew 7:3: "Don't pick on people, jump on their failures, criticize their faults—unless, of course, you want the same treatment" (msg).

> *Dear God, help me always remember that as long as there are humans and this earth exists, there will be sin. Help me deal with my sin as strongly as I complain about the sins of others. Help me offer mercy in the same way I am grateful for Your mercy. Amen.*

### Challenge

When you hear about sin in the lives of others, consider an alternative to gossip and criticism (hint: it's the subject of this book).

### Reflection

Why does it seem easier to pay attention to the faults of others than personal sin?

Why do you think God wants you to show mercy to others?

## Thursday—Evening

No one handles rejection very well. A man asking a woman for a date would rather not ask if he feels there is a chance of rejection. Some would opt to remain alone rather than to feel the sharp pain of rejection. Jesus knows rejection only too well. In a friendship with Jesus, the only rejection happens when someone rejects Him.

*Dear God, I am grateful that Your Son, Jesus, accepts me.*
*I am sorry when I act as if He will respond the way others*
*do. Help me remember that Your love rescues the rejected*
*and I never have to hide from You. Amen.*

### CHALLENGE

Consider the possibility that because God accepts you He wants you to accept others through His love, by His mercy, and for His glory.

### REFLECTION

Everyone has been rejected at some point. What feelings did you experience and what emotions were inspired from rejection?

God accepts you. What questions come to mind when you read those three words?

*Week 4: Friday*

# A MISUSED SECOND CHANCE

*Then Jonah prayed to his God from the belly of the fish.
He prayed: "In trouble, deep trouble, I prayed to GOD. He
answered me. From the belly of the grave I cried, 'Help!'"*
JONAH 2:1–2 MSG

Jonah was a prophet. He was supposed to speak for God. Yet when he was told where to deliver a message, Jonah hopped on a ship going the opposite direction. He didn't like God's message. If he actually delivered the message, it could mean that people he didn't like would get a second chance with God. If they never heard the message, maybe they'd never get the second chance. Jonah liked that idea.

While Jonah was avoiding mail service, God was stirring the appetite of an enormous fish. God brought a storm and Jonah found himself in the sea. That hungry fish provided the *time-out* Jonah needed.

Jonah had time to think. He had time to repent and inside a fish, Jonah prayed.

You should know that after that experience, the message was delivered. However, after the people accepted a second chance, Jonah forgot his own second chance and began to complain about the fairness of God.

This is an important part of praying through troubled times. Prayer is part of God's plan to transform you. When the struggle is your own fault, God wants you to learn from it and reject what sent you offtrack.

## *Friday—Morning*

It could be easy to feel disrespect for Jonah. If he had just obeyed, the story would have been so much better. Right? Jonah's story is useful because it's a lot like the story of most people. Mercy is the personal request, and justice toward others is the outward display. What God gives is not what's passed along. You may be able to connect with Jonah's prayer and actions.

*Dear God, when I'm going through struggles I am praying for me. I need help and I recognize You are the one to turn to in a crisis. When you show me mercy, even after I've created my own mess, help me remember how that mercy changed me, and help me find ways to be merciful to others. Amen.*

### Challenge

Think of three other words that are companions to mercy. Find ways to use these characteristics in the way you deal with other people.

### Reflection

Because you have received mercy from God, whom will you show mercy to today?

How does love for other people change the way you pray for them?

## Friday—Noon

The phrase "second chance" suggests you intend to do your best with a new opportunity that's offered. What happens when you blow it? God gives you another chance, but the goal of His mercy isn't abuse of His goodwill, but an acceptance of His plan. It's less a *forgiveness fill-up* and more of an *obedience offering*. He will be with you in a crisis of your own making, so honor the gift of His companionship.

*Dear God, give me the vision to see that when facing a crisis I've created, Your desire is to draw me close and point me in a direction that doesn't lead back to this crisis. Help me stop walking familiar paths when they keep leading away from You. Amen.*

### CHALLENGE

Spend some time thinking about something you do that keeps you from staying close to God. Consider any remedies you may have discovered so far and give them a try as you continue praying.

### REFLECTION

Describe some emotions you've felt when you recognized you'd been given a second chance.
Why do you think second chances are so important?

## Friday—Evening

Running away from God is an internal response to what you've experienced from human interactions. If you mess up, you may stay away from God because you're embarrassed or ashamed. If you walk the other way you might feel as if you've blown it so badly that God doesn't want anything to do with you. Because you stay away from God, you might just stay away from His people.

*Dear God, I need You. I struggle to live life by myself, and every time I try to do things without You I am reminded that once I recognize I need help, You make it available. Help me recognize it sooner. Amen.*

### CHALLENGE

Write down instances when you're certain God helped you through a crisis even though you had no reason to expect it. If you can remember your response, write this down beside each entry.

### REFLECTION

When you're ashamed, how does your relationship with God change?

If you really believed that God accepts you without condition, how would it change your prayer life?

# CRISIS MANAGEMENT

*Come close to God, and God will come close to you.*
*Wash your hands, you sinners; purify your hearts,*
*for your loyalty is divided between God and the world.*
JAMES 4:8 NLT

Struggles come from many places: the choices others make, the ones you make, times of testing, and moments of temptation. Each requires prayer, but what you pray for will be different in each situation.

God wants you to pray in a crisis, but your relationship with Him, before the crisis, can impact the final solution. In every circumstance the reason to pray should be to discover the closeness you've always wanted with the God who made you for relationship.

Being divided between God's answer to your crisis and society's suggestion to never give God top billing can test your loyalty and extend your crisis. When the people of Israel struggled with divided loyalty, Joshua spoke and put everything in perspective: "If you refuse to serve the LORD, then choose today whom you will serve. . . . As for me and my family, we will serve the LORD" (Joshua 24:15 NLT).

A crisis can be a reminder of what's important, an invitation to come home, a call to action, a neon sign of relationship, and a plea for purity.

When you struggle, God is moving. Nothing good is

ever accomplished without the stress between where you are and where God wants you to be. The struggle means God has something better for you. His ultimate call is much like His challenge to the disciples: "Come, follow me" (Matthew 4:19 NLT). This is a challenge worth accepting.

## *Saturday—Morning*

You have a choice in whom you follow. One choice is God. The other choice is anyone opposed to God (the Bible calls this choice "the world"). Some advice can be found in 1 John 2:16: "Practically everything that goes on in the world—wanting your own way, wanting everything for yourself, wanting to appear important—has nothing to do with the Father. It just isolates you from him" (MSG).

*Dear God, following You is a greater choice than following anyone or anything else. Praying to You is a sign of my allegiance, a symbol of my trust, and a pledge of my companionship. Thank You for loving me first so I know how to love You in return. Amen.*

### CHALLENGE

Take some time to think about how you relate to God. Honestly evaluate where He fits on your priority list.

### REFLECTION

Name three attributes you always associate with God. Name three attributes you always associate with society.

## Saturday—Noon

*Society's suggestion* is often that of a bully who wants to minimize the importance of God in the lives of His children. Listen long enough and you'll hear that God is not relevant, would seek to enslave you in a ridiculous set of rules, or that He is the product of your imagination. God's answer? Hebrews 11:6 says, "Anyone who wants to approach God must believe both that he exists and that he cares enough to respond to those who seek him" (MSG).

> *Dear God, because You exist, I exist. Because You exist,*
> *I can come to You boldly in prayer. Because You exist,*
> *I can trust You to respond to my questions. Because You*
> *exist, I will seek You. You exist. I believe it. Amen.*

### CHALLENGE

Develop a list that features the many ways people try to deny the existence of God.

### REFLECTION

Why do you think it takes faith to believe in God?
How do you think prayer can enhance your faith in God?

*Saturday—Evening*

A crisis can remind you that there is only one successful exit strategy. When you deal with struggles alone, you can expect deep wounds and faith reduction. When you rely on God to walk you through the struggle, remember He's the Great Physician, Healer, and Helper. When you have a crisis, God brings control.

> *Dear God, when I have a crisis You deliver*
> *everything I can't. Your hope helps me hang on.*
> *Your mercy overwhelms me. Your love inspires*
> *cooperation. In the middle of personal struggle,*
> *I realize once more why I need a Savior.*
> *I remember Your faithfulness even when I am*
> *unfaithful. You leave me in awe. Amen.*

#### CHALLENGE

Take the information you learned last week about God's will and combine it with this week's content on praying through difficult times. Consider how they connect.

#### REFLECTION

Why do you think struggling alone leaves you with deeper personal wounds?

How do you think a crisis can be used to increase faith?

# HEARING GOD THROUGH PRAYER

*We may expect answers to prayer, and should not be easy without them any more than we should be if we had written a letter to a friend upon important business, and had received no reply.*
CHARLES SPURGEON

You send an important text, but there's no reply. You send an e-mail with specific concerns, but the respondent only returns a vague greeting with no answers. You ask someone a question and they skirt it without ever saying what you wanted to hear. Frustration is your companion.

When you ask God a question, you have a strong connection to the moment He gives an answer. Is it possible you're listening for His answer in all the wrong places? Is it possible you have misunderstood how He answers? Is it possible you're waiting for an audible voice? If you answered yes to any of these questions, this week is for you.

The week starts with *never give up* prayers. These are prayers that require a bold heart that believes enough in their request to keep praying when the answer seems slow in delivery.

Today's greatest spoiler alert is that God answers prayers and He will speak to you, but rarely with an audible voice. You may need to alter your understanding of the word "speak" if you want to hear what God is saying to you.

You'll explore the lives of two men in the Bible who actually heard God's voice and will follow the circumstances that lead to this level of conversation with God.

Each day you can explore ways that God speaks to His people, and you'll uncover a warning or two about who might seem to be speaking for God, but their message should not be believed (Matthew 7:21).

Every twenty-four hours you'll have an opportunity to refine your prayer life to gain the most from every private conversation with God.

In those moments when God's Word doesn't make sense, you should know that God has given you a study partner who can help you understand what He's saying (1 Corinthians 2:14), what He wants from you (Micah 6:8), and how it's possible to follow Him completely (Psalm 119:11).

God has answers to your questions. Keep asking, seeking, and knocking until the answer comes, your search is over, and the door is opened (Luke 11:9). As you've learned already, not every answer will follow your preconceived solution. God may answer in a way you never expected. He may lead through unfamiliar places. His love for you is stronger than whether you agree with His answer.

Hearing God's voice isn't the result of following a magical formula or being a modern-day spiritual superhero. This week, you'll discover that *anyone* in God's family can hear His voice. Your response plays a key role in whether the conversation continues. The biggest question you may need to wrestle with is whether you will listen when God speaks.

# THE PRAYERS OF
# THE PERSISTENT

*One day Jesus told his disciples a story to show
that they should always pray and never give up.*
Luke 18:1 NLT

Prayer can be an exercise in persistence. Jesus was a master storyteller, and it showed up in a parable about a widow who was unrelenting in pursuing justice for herself. The judge did not have a reputation for compassion, he lacked the ability to be considerate, and his attitude was that of *I just don't care.*

He ignored the widow, but when she kept showing up each day to plead for justice there came a point when the judge gave in. Verse 5 says, "This woman is driving me crazy. I'm going to see that she gets justice, because she is wearing me out with her constant requests!" (NLT).

Was Jesus comparing an unjust judge with God? No. He was comparing the outcome of those who are persistent in their prayers with those who are not. Verse 7 asks rhetorical questions that put persistence in perspective: "Don't you think God will surely give justice to his chosen people who cry out to him day and night? Will he keep putting them off?" (NLT).

The contrast is that an unjust judge can be motivated to render a just verdict, but a just God always has an interest in setting things right for His family.

When you need something from God, ask specifically and persistently. Have a faith-filled conviction that only God can answer this prayer. His answer is heard when genuine needs are met.

*Sunday—Morning*

Persistence in prayer can grow your faith. When you pray believing God can and will answer your prayer, then you don't give up when you aren't given an immediate answer. If God is saying, "Wait," then your persistence continues to promote a personal interest in His answer.

*Dear God, I'm learning that I can come to You boldly and pray persistently for something I really need. You give good gifts, and You give me what I ask for or something much better. Let me always be grateful for Your better answers to my persistent prayers. Amen.*

## Challenge

Think about a time when someone came to you with something they needed help with. Write down your response and whether it was more like the judge or God.

## Reflection

How are you challenged when it comes to thinking you might be bothering God with your prayers?

What connection can you think of between faith and
persistent prayer?

*Sunday—Noon*

The purpose of persistent prayer isn't to annoy God or to
nag. God knows what you need, and His answer is always
perfect. Your persistent prayer keeps you aligned with
the One you recognize as fully able to meet your need. A
persistent prayer says you haven't changed your mind, you
haven't forgotten the One who answers, and you believe
His answer is on the way.

*Dear God, at the end of my "never give up" prayer, help me
recognize Your answer, praise You for Your compassionate
gift, and honor You in the answer You give. You love me,
and the timing of Your answer is just right, even when
I think I needed it yesterday. Amen.*

### CHALLENGE

If you've prayed persistently for something in the past,
write down your experience.

### REFLECTION

How does praying persistently remind you of trying to
overcome a struggle?
When you pray persistently it can be easy to think God
owes you the answer you want. How can you resist
this kind of thinking?

## Sunday—Evening

Persistent prayer is passionate prayer. It doesn't automatically settle for an "if you get around to it" perspective. It is a prayer of faith. There is no sway in the thinking of the one who prays. If it's important to you, then it's important to God. His love will be evident in what He knows will be best for you.

*Dear God, my persistent prayer could be wrapped up in my dreams for my life, my hopes for others, a physical need, or a decision I need to make. In my persistence, help me also discover the patience to wait for Your answer. Amen.*

### Challenge

When you're praying a persistent prayer, take the time to do some research. Explore the Bible to see if there may be any reasons why God might answer with a no. If not, keep praying.

### Reflection

By persistently praying, do you think God will answer with a yes to prayers that ask for something He has said is off-limits? Why or why not?

How important is it that your prayers match the purpose of His Word?

*Week 5: Monday*

# HOW SERIOUSLY ARE
# YOU LISTENING?

*Good friend, take to heart what I'm telling you; collect my
counsels and guard them with your life. Tune your ears to the
world of Wisdom; set your heart on a life of Understanding.
That's right—if you make Insight your priority, and won't
take no for an answer, searching for it like a prospector
panning for gold, like an adventurer on a treasure hunt,
believe me, before you know it Fear-of-GOD will be yours;
you'll have come upon the Knowledge of God.*

PROVERBS 2:1–5 MSG

If you claim you want God's will for your life but refuse to
read His words in the Bible, then your claim may be less a
product of faith and more a case of building on the sands
of wishful thinking. The heart of God is found in the pages
of a book much older than you.

Pray without reading the Bible and it can seem like
your prayers are returned as undeliverable. Pray without
God's Word to guide you and you're on a long journey
without a map. Pray without the support of God's
answers and your faith will diminish because you have no
information that's truly acceptable and trustworthy.

You have to decide if you really want to hear God's
answers. Listening means paying attention. You'll learn
things you never knew. You could read God's Word and
get a front-row seat to His answers.

If you refuse to read God's Word, you might need to determine how serious you are about wanting God to answer your prayers.

## *Monday—Morning*

Jesus said in Luke 11:28, "Blessed are those who hear God's Word and guard it with their lives!" (MSG). Spiritual hearing can come through your ears, but it can also come through your eyes. Your mind can receive the words and accept the answers. Those who take steps toward really hearing what God has to say through His Word are called "blessed."

*Dear God, I want to be blessed by You. I want to listen to Your Words through what was written in Your Book, the Bible. Help me remember the value of hearing Your desires for my life through the Bible. Amen.*

### CHALLENGE

Think back on your prayer life to when your prayers were least effective. Consider how much time you spent reading the Bible.

### REFLECTION

Name two ways your prayer life could improve by reading the Bible.

What is your greatest challenge in spending time in God's Word?

*Monday—Noon*

Proverbs 4:21–22 says, "Keep my message in plain view at all times. Concentrate! Learn it by heart! Those who discover these words live, really live" (MSG). When you have instructions for life, it just makes sense for you to "really live." Often the Bible is set aside as a sacred text for church service, thought of as lacking what's needed for everyday living. Let this sink in: God's Word doesn't have an expiration date, and it's not confined to a geographical location.

*Dear God, my spiritual vision improves the more time I spend reading Your Word. Let it be as important to me as air, water, and food. May I keep Your message in plain view, and may I spend enough time in the Bible that I remember Your Words even when I'm not reading them. Amen.*

**CHALLENGE**

Look up three verses that deal with God's Word. Take the one that is most meaningful to you, write it down, and memorize it.

**REFLECTION**

In the verse above, you saw the word *concentrate*.
  Why do you think it is so hard to concentrate in today's culture?
What can you do to minimize distractions when you're reading God's Word?

## *Monday—Evening*

Psalm 19:11 says, "God's Word warns us of danger and directs us to hidden treasure. Otherwise how will we find our way? Or know when we play the fool?" (msg). Read the Bible and find guidance. Read the Bible and discover wisdom. Concentrate and uncover spiritual treasure.

*Dear God, I don't always think of Your Word as a treasure map, a key to avoid danger, or a life compass. May I spend time learning from You within the pages of Your Book. Amen.*

### CHALLENGE

Write down five ways you could describe God's Word.

### REFLECTION

When it comes to prayer, why should there be a balance between sharing your heart with God and reading His Word?

How can reading God's Word show growth in your prayer life?

*Week 5: Tuesday*

# A VOICE SPEAKING

*How can they call on him to save them unless they
believe in him? And how can they believe in him
if they have never heard about him? And how can
they hear about him unless someone tells them?*

Romans 10:14 nlt

God gave the gift of preaching and teaching to many
within His family. Men and women speak a message to
those who need to hear it most. In the Old Testament,
God used prophets to define His will, describe His
commands, and detail the future of those who listened.

Today, you can hear from God through radio, podcasts, in church, and in the printed word. There is one
thing to remember: no matter what you hear or read from
others you still need to go back to God's Word to see
if it matches what God said. Second Timothy 4:3 says,
"For a time is coming when people will no longer listen
to sound and wholesome teaching. They will follow their
own desires and will look for teachers who will tell them
whatever their itching ears want to hear" (nlt).

God has always used people to share His message,
but He has no use for those who intentionally lead others
to wrong. You need other Christians and the hope their
words can inspire, so get together with them regularly
(Hebrews 10:25).

God is perfect—mankind is not. Follow up what you

learn from others by checking the Bible. When mistakes are made in sharing God's message, they can be corrected by the Bible.

## *Tuesday—Morning*

Everyone is affected by the words others speak. Consider the impact of your words. Ephesians 4:29 says, "Let everything you say be good and helpful, so that your words will be an encouragement to those who hear them" (NLT). God can speak to others through you, which is strong encouragement to know Him better.

*Dear God, when it comes to sharing You with others, help me never make up a good answer when I don't really know for sure. Give me the courage to seek Your Word and learn what I need to know to truly answer the questions others ask. May my words point to You. Amen.*

### CHALLENGE

Write down an example of how God's Word has changed the way you once thought about something.

### REFLECTION

How important is it to use the Bible as the source for correct(ed) thinking?

What should you do when what you think is different than what the Bible says is truth?

## Tuesday—Noon

Many will experience the sense that they have heard from God while listening to someone speak. This can be a God designed transfer of information, encouragement, and support. It's helpful, welcome, and affirming. God speaks through the words, actions, and life choices of His people. But with knowledge comes a greater sense of purpose and responsibility.

*Dear God, I'm grateful that the words You wrote have encouraged others. I'm better for finding people who share that encouragement with me. Help me take their life investment and reinvest in others. Amen.*

### CHALLENGE

God's design is to encourage people with His Word, will, and wisdom. Write down some ways you can pass these on.

### REFLECTION

What you do reflects your relationship with God.
  How is your reflection?
How have the words of other Christians influenced
  your view of God?

## Tuesday—Evening

The Old Testament prophets spoke a message God gave to them. Many were imprisoned, harmed, or exiled for sharing the truth. God's message isn't always well received or immediately accepted. God's message can be heard through your voice or the voices of others, but it may cause some to be upset with the message and the messenger.

*Dear God, thank You for bringing people into my life who are willing to be used to share a message with me. Help me accept Your truth and use it to identify error. Help me appreciate the message and love the Author of truth. Keep me returning to Your Word and storing it within the core of my being to help me when I have spiritual memory loss. Amen.*

### CHALLENGE

Consider how growing in community with other Christians can inspire learning, sharing, and thriving in your walk with God. Journal your thoughts and share them with at least one other Christian.

### REFLECTION

How do you think God can use discipleship to share His message with you?

Why do Christians need to grow in their faith as opposed to immediately knowing everything God wants them to know?

*Week 5: Wednesday*

## CIRCUMSTANTIAL ANSWERS

*[God said,] "I know what I'm doing. I have it all planned out—plans to take care of you, not abandon you, plans to give you the future you hope for."*
JEREMIAH 29:11 MSG

It's possible to recognize God's voice in everyday events, but for many His voice is only recognized in stories of divine faithfulness and intervention after the fact.

God orchestrated circumstances so an unjustly imprisoned Joseph would be in the right place at the right time to save His family (Genesis 50:20), He took care of all the details for a blind man who needed to be healed by Jesus (Mark 8:22–25), and God is perfectly willing to write your faith story, too (Hebrews 12:2).

You shouldn't be surprised when you pass through circumstances without realizing you're witnessing God's answer to your prayer. When you take the time to remember the past, you're witness to a clear message from God. His faithfulness took the ordinary and transformed it into nothing short of a miracle.

Focusing on past circumstances that only God could link to real-life answers brings praise to your prayer life, perspective to your present crisis, and trust in His ultimate answer.

As with any method you use to hear God's answer, remember God will never direct you in a way that contradicts His Word. If you believe God is telling you to do something His Word calls sin, then you can be sure you're listening to the wrong voice.

Trust scripture; God knows what He's doing, and He won't ask you to do something that contradicts His word.

## *Wednesday—Morning*

Your circumstances never surprise God. He can work in every environment. He can use encouragement from a friend, a new job, or even lack of money to bring you to a greater sense of trust in His plans. You may not think you hear His voice, but it could be a whisper that gently says, *"Follow Me. It's time to move."*

*Dear God, thank You for keeping me where I am or moving me to where I need to be. Help me recognize Your voice through Your actions. Help me see that the circumstances I'm in can draw me closer to Your plan. Amen.*

### CHALLENGE

Try thinking of someplace where God is not. Read Psalm 139 for ideas. Write down your thoughts.

### REFLECTION

Have you ever felt God turned His back on you?
    Do you still feel that way? Why or why not?
What evidence can you think of that shows God is
    speaking to you?

## Wednesday—Noon

In 1 Kings 19, the prophet Elijah was in a bad place emotionally. The king was after him, and Elijah told God he was ready to die in order to be done with the trouble he faced. Elijah's dejected circumstances had him facing high winds, earthquake, and fire. When everything grew quiet, Elijah heard God in a whisper. Sometimes it's not the big events that point to God's voice. Sometimes you just need to be quiet enough to listen.

*Dear God, people say that it's the little things that count. Apparently You think so, too. It can be easy for me to overlook the good things You've done. While I'm looking for big signs advertising Your plan, the path I'm walking is filled with the accumulated goodness that You send to refresh my journey. Thank You. Amen.*

### CHALLENGE

Write down one small thing you can remember that was instrumental in moving you toward God's plan. Include some of the things that continued to change for the best after this simple event.

### REFLECTION

Why do you think God spoke to Elijah in a whisper? What do you think you miss by not paying attention to the small things God takes care of every day?

*Wednesday—Evening*

When God speaks to you through many small answers to a bigger problem, it can feel like you're being given time-released puzzle pieces that will connect to provide a clear picture of His plan. You can't always tell what you're looking at from a single piece, but in the end you might find yourself drawing in a breath of awe at what you discover, and finding reason to praise God through what you learned.

*Dear God, help me take each small answer You provide and joyfully fit it together with Your other answers to understand You better. Help me see this adventure as a way to draw close to You in the midst of daily battles. I just live better with You by my side. Amen.*

### CHALLENGE

Write out the phrase, "God loves me." Spend time thinking about how each small word connects with the other two words to create a profound truth. Use this as a reminder that small things can connect to create a bigger picture.

### REFLECTION

Why do you think most people want God to speak to them using big signs?
Why do you think God typically shares His plan in small pieces?

# YOUR STUDY PARTNER

*[Jesus said], "The Helper, the Holy Spirit, whom the Father will send in My name, He will teach you all things, and bring to your remembrance all things that I said to you."*
JOHN 14:26 NKJV

There's a reason the psalmist said, "I've banked your promises in the vault of my heart so I won't sin myself bankrupt" (Psalm 119:11 MSG). Knowing what God actually says and then thinking about it, memorizing it, and praying about it places God's answers deep in your *heart vault of God's promises.*

This is where the Holy Spirit can speak to you. He's the Helper, Teacher, and Companion that Jesus promised to those who follow Him. He reminds you of the things you've learned, sends up red flags when you're walking away from God's plan, and He instructs. If He instructs, then expect Him to speak. Perhaps His words will not be audible, but they will be clear and will always mirror what you're learning in the Bible.

Romans 15:13 says, "May the God of hope fill you with all joy and peace in believing, that you may abound in hope by the power of the Holy Spirit" (NKJV). When you struggle, when you pray, when you need hope, remember that every Christian has the Holy Spirit to remind them of God's love, faithfulness, and plan. The hope He gives is the assurance you need that God is still working things out for your good and His honor.

The more time you spend studying God's Word with the companionship of the Holy Spirit, the clearer His voice becomes.

*Thursday—Morning*

The Holy Spirit is God's gift to His family. Ezekiel 36:26 says, "I will give you a new heart and put a new spirit within you; I will take the heart of stone out of your flesh and give you a heart of flesh" (NKJV). He is the perfect remedy for a jaded response, sarcastic tongue, and unforgiving spirit. He takes fractured minds and hearts. In their place He leaves something less like the person you were and more like the God who rescues, speaks life, and offers hope.

*Dear God, thank You for the gift of Your Spirit.*
*Help me listen when He speaks, think when He teaches,*
*and enjoy His companionship. Thank You for never*
*leaving me alone and for clearing up my confusion.*
*Thanks for making me more like You. Amen.*

#### CHALLENGE

Write down an instance when you believed God was speaking to you through His Spirit. What did He say? How did you respond?

Why do you think it can be hard to believe the Holy
Spirit speaks to you?

Can you think of any circumstances where the Spirit
would remain silent? If so, what would they be?

## *Thursday—Noon*

The Holy Spirit seems the most free to speak when
Christians read God's Word. When Jesus was being
tempted in the wilderness He said something that's
important to your spiritual health. Matthew 4:4 says,
"It is written, 'Man shall not live by bread alone, but by
every word that proceeds from the mouth of God'" (NKJV).
Discover the feast that is God's Word.

*Dear God, teach me, prepare me, encourage me. I don't want
to guess, create theories, or settle for opinions. Show me in
Your Word and speak to me through the Holy Spirit so I can
see clearly, hope deeply, and follow faithfully. Amen.*

**CHALLENGE**

Write down the one thing you most want to know from
God. Pray, keep investing time in God's Word, and track
what you learn.

**REFLECTION**

What role have you thought the Holy Spirit played in
your life?

How has today's reading challenged your perception of
  God's Spirit?

## Thursday—Evening

Today's verse says that the Holy Spirit will teach us "all
things." If you're like most people you think of God and
you think of Jesus. You know the Holy Spirit is part of the
triune nature of God, but you might not think of Him in
the same way you do the first two. He is no less God—
He's your teacher. He even intercedes for you when you
don't have the words to pray (Romans 8:26–27).

*Dear God, since Your Spirit is willing to teach, help me be
willing to learn. Since He is willing to be my advocate, help me
follow His advice. Since He is part of You, help me give Him
honor and pay attention when He has something to say. Amen.*

### CHALLENGE

List three things you believe the Holy Spirit has taught
you about God. If you're a new Christian, fill in the
blanks when He *does* teach.

### REFLECTION

How would you describe the Holy Spirit?
How does it feel to know you have God's Spirit as
  your teacher?

# READY TO LISTEN

*Then GOD came and stood before him exactly as before,*
*calling out, "Samuel! Samuel!" Samuel answered,*
*"Speak. I'm your servant, ready to listen."*
1 SAMUEL 3:10 MSG

Samuel was a young boy serving in Israel's temple. His life had been offered as a gift to God by his mother, Hannah. Samuel would grow to be the prophet to Israel's first kings. But in these early years he didn't recognize God's voice. It was the priest Eli who helped Samuel come to terms with the fact that God was speaking.

Once Samuel proved willing to listen and able to understand what God was saying, he was used for decades to share God's message with God's people. Samuel heard some hard things, repeated those hard things, and wasn't always the most popular guy for doing so.

When you ask God to speak to you through His Word, Spirit, or circumstances, you might consider rejecting what He says, but if you enjoy a close relationship with God, it's never in your best interest to refuse to obey what He tells you.

There's much to learn from the last few words of verse 10. Samuel asked God to speak because he believed He could. Samuel referred to himself as a servant because he recognized the leadership of God. Samuel gave God a gift by indicating he was ready to listen.

When you don't hear God speak, it could be that you don't believe He will, you want to do things your own way, or you're not willing to listen. If any of these are true for you, there might be a reason for God's silence.

## Friday—Morning

Samuel had access to a *voice to ear* conversation most never experience. You might think Samuel just accepted the fact God was speaking as if it were an everyday experience. However, it may also be possible that a young boy was anxious knowing that the God he served had a message He wanted to personally share with him.

*Dear God, help me believe that You actually speak and that if I'm to understand what You want, I will need to listen. I will need to obey. I will need to serve Your interests over my own. Speak, I'm Your servant, ready to listen. Amen.*

### CHALLENGE

Consider how unbelievable it must have sounded to Samuel that God was actually speaking to him. Describe how you think you might have felt if you were Samuel.

### REFLECTION

Would you be surprised if God spoke directly to your need? Why or why not?
Why is it hard to believe that you can actually know God's thoughts on issues that challenge you?

### Friday—Noon

It's possible for God to speak through His Word, Spirit, and circumstances, and what He says might be something you don't want to hear. You might think, "*Anything but that, God.*" You serve a God who's called Truth. If you don't like what He says, you need to consider whether a human or the Truthmaker is right.

*Dear God, it is easy to accept Your truth when it's what I want to hear. When my will conflicts with Yours, help me realize Your answers are not only a response to my prayers but a call to follow directions that may take me out of my comfort zone. Help me accept even the hard answers. Amen.*

#### CHALLENGE

Consider whether you really believe God's Word has God's answers. Consider how that should affect your life decisions.

#### REFLECTION

When did you last pray seeking God's comfort, without wanting Him to get involved in the decision making?
Why do you think prayer, scripture reading, and obedience are all linked?

## Friday—Evening

When you pray, there may be times when it seems God is silent. If God has answered earlier prayers and you haven't done what He's asked, it's probable that He won't trust you with more answers until you're faithful with acting on answers He's already given.

*Dear God, obedience is hard when it conflicts with my personal plans. Help me remove any obstacles to new answers by doing what You've already asked me to do. Give me the strength to do what needs to be done. Help me admit when I've blown it. And in Your forgiveness, help me walk forward with Your plan once more. Amen.*

### CHALLENGE

Consider the role you might play in how God answers prayer. Consider one thing you can do today to make it easier for God to answer your prayers.

### REFLECTION

Why do you think it's so hard to obey God while still wanting Him to answer prayers?

If you knew God's answers before you asked a question, do you think that knowledge would change your personal obedience to His plan? Why or why not?

*Week 5: Saturday*

# THE FRIEND OF GOD

*The LORD would speak to Moses face to face,
as one speaks to a friend.*
EXODUS 33:11 NIV

Moses wasn't the first man God spoke to "face to face," but there was something uncommon about the conversations God had with him. God spoke to Moses from a burning bush (Exodus 3), in the tabernacle (Numbers 7:89), and from atop Mount Sinai (Exodus 19).

The Bible provides an answer as to why it was easy for Moses to speak to God, and for God to speak to His servant. Numbers 12:3 says, "Now Moses was a very humble man, more humble than anyone else on the face of the earth" (NIV).

Moses didn't come to God with a personal agenda for God to approve. Moses came to God in humility and trust. The agenda Moses followed was God's agenda. God took a man willing to obey and created one of the most dynamic conversations in scripture. The only conversation more remarkable was God's conversation with His Son, Jesus.

God even took the time to explain that He actually spoke to Moses. God said in Numbers 12:6–7, "When there is a prophet among you, I, the LORD, reveal myself to them in visions, I speak to them in dreams. But this is not true of my servant Moses; he is faithful in all my house" (NIV).

The lives of Moses and Jesus prove instructional when it comes to hearing God's voice. Their prayers were not casual, but filled with belief, honored God above all, and had the assurance that God had real answers for people living in uncertain times.

## Saturday—Morning

Christians can be guilty of lobbying God for their own pet projects. Like a debate team in their element, Christians can give a five-point plan on why their idea has the greatest chance for success. God is not often consulted in the making of the plan, and there can be an unmistakable sense that the only answer accepted is God's agreement to the plans of people. If you were really smarter than God, why would you need Him? The truth is God knows everything and you *do* need Him.

*Dear God, help me resist the urge to dictate terms in my relationship with You. You've never needed to consult any human to come up with the right solution. Forgive me when I arrogantly believe You need my help in a crisis. May I trust You more, and my solutions less. Amen.*

### CHALLENGE

Write down a time when you believed you didn't need to consult God because you felt you already knew the answer. Consider what you learned as a result.

When you experience difficulty in life, is your first
response to try to fix it yourself or to ask God for
help? Why?

In your experience, who has the greatest solutions
to the problems you face? Explain.

*Saturday—Noon*

Moses didn't start out humble. God placed Moses in the
home of the pharaoh and he was treated like royalty. He
was entitled and perhaps a little spoiled. He took matters
into his own hands without consulting God (Exodus 2),
and a single decision put him in the wilderness for forty
years while God waited for the right set of circumstances
to deliver Moses to the threshold of humility.

*Dear God, I don't want it to take forty years for me to
humble myself enough to call on You first. Help me learn
from Moses and see You as the First-Responder to my
needs. Teach me to stop wasting time with solutions
that don't bear Your approval. Amen.*

**CHALLENGE**

List three practical ways you can turn the spotlight from
where you're standing to where God is working.

**REFLECTION**

Why do you think God finds humility a positive trait
in His people?

Why do you think humility is such a difficult trait to acquire?

## Saturday—Evening

Hearing God is what you want, but a lack of faithfulness causes spiritual deafness. The further you drift from God the harder it is to hear His voice. The usual places where you can hear Him are rarely visited. While you carry on a one-sided conversation in prayer, you have effectively stopped listening to His answer with a closed Bible, crippled heart, and divided mind.

*Dear God, I know You're faithful to me, but there are days I don't feel loyal. I keep moving out of earshot of Your whisper. I ask for Your help and tune out every offer of help You send my way. I don't want to run; I don't want to hide. I don't want to be without our divine conversation. Bring me back to the place where I recognize the whisper of Your voice. Amen.*

### CHALLENGE

Write down as many things as you can think of that change within you when you walk away from God's will.

### REFLECTION

How is walking apart from God similar to running away from home? How are they different?
What one thought today challenged you the most?

# THE PAGES OF PRAYER MODEL

*Fear not because your prayer is stammering, your words feeble, and your language poor. Jesus can understand you.*
J. C. RYLE

This is a week of exceptionally good news if you have wanted to know what kind of prayer pleases God. The quick answer? Any kind that recognizes His ability to help.

Maybe you want a prayer that feels a bit like a recipe. You want instructions that include all the right ingredients, how long to bake the prayer, and at what temperature. Just like your favorite recipe, you know there has to be a combination of individual tastes that results in something that satisfies.

The *PAGES of prayer model* is one of many prayer models that identifies some of the most powerful reasons to pray and combines them with the impact these individual ideas have had in the prayer lives of people you can read about in God's Word. Monday through Friday of this week will take you through each letter of the prayer model and give plenty of opportunity to apply it to your prayer life.

There is no magic here, and a prayer formula *can* result in a stale prayer life when it becomes ritual instead of revelation, but it doesn't have to.

This prayer model is included because it's practical, biblical, and can boost *prayer life confidence*. However, there's no substitute for authentic, transparent, and genuine prayer, so you shouldn't look at this prayer model as the beginning and end of your search for positive prayer. It's called a *model* for a reason.

Like an architect, this plan pulls together prayer design goals and crafts the blueprints to build a prayer. Like a chef, there are ingredients here that lead to good taste in *God conversation*. Like an auto mechanic, this type of prayer can keep your spiritual engine running at levels of optimal efficiency.

But any prayer model will only work when prayer itself remains a matter of the heart and not just a product of the mind. This means that if you go through each letter in this model and simply say what you think God wants to hear, instead of reflecting how each element really looks in the core of who you are, then you might think this model has failed.

If it fails, it may be that holy prayer has turned into little more than a checklist. It can be like reading a church bulletin to know how many things still need to happen before you can go home. There is no joy, insight, or engagement when a model prayer becomes a to-do list.

Now that you recognize the challenge, there are actually many great reasons to celebrate this prayer model. It can provide a training ground if you're just learning to pray. It can be a refresher course if your prayer life has grown stale. It can be an encouragement if you just want to grow deeper in your conversations with God.

Refuse to let prayer become routine while you consider a prayer model that can infuse power into each new conversation with God.

# SIDESHOW PRAYERS

*When you come before God, don't turn that into a
theatrical production either. All these people making
a regular show out of their prayers, hoping for stardom!
Do you think God sits in a box seat?*
MATTHEW 6:5 MSG

Jesus observed people praying, but it came across like a low-rent theatrical production. Their hearts weren't connected to God. Their minds were only interested in impressing anyone willing to listen. The prayers were memorized, recited with a flourish, and their voices changed in an attempt to elicit an emotional response from people who were either unimpressed or intimidated.

There's no doubt God wants you to pray with others, but He doesn't want you to forget the reason for prayer. It's not to move people emotionally—it's a conversation with God. It's not to earn brownie points—it's to learn what God wants. It's not to improve social standing—it's to learn how to stand when falling becomes far too easy.

Everyone feels insignificant in some way. *Everyone.* Some will settle for the satisfaction and pride of a prayer well prayed instead of a prayer offered in humble transparency. The first response might impress people, but it's the second that gets God's attention and invites His conversation.

God knows you're fragile and have all kinds of

needs (Psalm 103:14). He knows you're broken and need mending (Isaiah 64:8), which is why bragging shouldn't factor into your prayers. He knows you want people to notice you, but drawing attention to yourself limits God's interest in working through you (Matthew 6:6). Impersonal prayers always keep God at a distance.

### Sunday—Morning

Prayer is not an Olympic sport with medals and media coverage. It's not a performance with a "best in show" medal at stake. It's not a competition with bragging rights for the winner. It can be hard to concentrate on who you're praying to when you're comparing your prayer with one offered by someone else.

*Dear God, it can be easy to think I need to pray differently in a group than I do when it's just You and I. Help me accept there's only One I'm speaking to when I pray with others. Help me remember I'm not on a stage with judges waiting to critique my performance. I'm Your child, and You understand me better than anyone. Thank You. Amen.*

#### CHALLENGE

Consider a time when you heard someone pray a sideshow prayer. Write down your impressions of that prayer.

Why do you think it's easy to think of prayer as a
performance?

Why is it easy to be critical of yourself when you think
your prayer doesn't measure up to others?

*Sunday—Noon*

You live in a world that resembles a playground and you're
wondering if you're going to be the last person picked for
another humiliating game. Admitting this can be painful
for an adult who believes they're well adjusted and over
that level of pettiness. When it comes to your relationship with God, His acceptance eliminates any need to
impress Him.

> *Dear God, I don't want to be that child who leaves
> a playground game wondering if I'm worth anything.
> Help me remember You made me, love me, and want to
> talk to me. Since I don't make a stage production out of talking
> to other people, help me speak plainly with You. Amen.*

CHALLENGE

Think back to a time when you were very uncomfortable
praying in a group. Write down your thoughts regarding
what made you uncomfortable.

What new insights in today's reading have left a
mark on your thinking?
What causes you to feel most insignificant? Why?

## Sunday—Evening

Today's reading suggested that "impersonal prayers always
keep God at a distance." Maybe it's because if you don't
believe what you're saying, then how can the God who
knows you accept a prayer that's less than genuine? If you
don't trust God enough to come to Him with your actual
need, you can expect very little conversation.

*Dear God, impersonal prayers seem to say that I don't
trust You enough to be honest with You. If I won't
share the deepest pain, greatest concern, and my genuine
needs, then I shouldn't expect You to truly answer them—
because I never actually told You what they were.
Keep me honest in prayer, Father. Amen.*

### CHALLENGE

Write a heartfelt prayer and an impersonal prayer. Note
the differences.

### REFLECTION

What might keep you from being honest with God?
What one thing can you do today to make your prayer
life more personal?

# *P* IS FOR PRAISE

*Oh come, let us worship and bow down;*
*let us kneel before the LORD our Maker.*
PSALM 95:6 NKJV

Praise can be a prayer, and prayer can be praise. The intent of the heart can make it so.

Praise is also the first word in the *PAGES of prayer model*. Each letter in PAGES can be used to improve your prayer life. Combine them for the greatest blessing.

The act of praise invites you to remember, and in the remembering count the multiple blessings God has attached to your story. Because God is good, it's important to add praise to prayers that request His help.

Praise isn't just for God. Praise moves you to a better way of thinking about the One to whom you pray.

Singing can be an act of praise and can be included in your prayers, but praise is ultimately the act of assigning worth to God. It's realizing you have access to something beyond understanding in your friendship with God. You're given access to wisdom, understanding, and answers. You have admittance to the throne room of the Creator, Redeemer, and Forgiver. He is more than you are, better than money, and His future includes you.

In moments of prayer you'll receive the gift of awe. This is something you can't manufacture, and may not even be able to understand. Awe helps you see God for who He is and helps you understand how much He loves you.

Begin your prayers with praise. It can change every other part of your prayer life.

*Monday—Morning*

The name of this prayer model is a constant reminder of where to turn first for God's answers. Each letter stands for something important to your life of prayer. The *PAGES of prayer model* always begin and end in the Bible. Praise plays a vital role in your prayer journey. Pray and read God's answers.

*Dear God, help me take the time to remember the ways You've already walked through difficulties with me. May my memories be clear enough to recall that I'd have been lost without Your help. May the praise that builds within me make each prayer time sweeter than the last. Amen.*

## CHALLENGE

Write a list of things that God has done for you in the past month. Stop and think about each time God helped you. Describe how remembering affects the way you relate to God today.

## REFLECTION

How do you think a lack of praise might affect your prayer life?
To what degree have you included praise in your prayers before today?

*Monday—Noon*

God has given the gift of memory. The reason the past is often referred to as "the good old days" is because the negative aspects of life are usually minimized while positive moments make your mental highlight reel. Perhaps God wants good memories of the past to instill a trust in His ability to manage the present and future. Remembering God's goodness is essential to praise.

*Dear God, thank You for the ability to remember the past and look forward to Your eternity. I want to remember that when difficult days came, Your grace arrived right on time. I want to remember Your goodness because my future is with You. Amen.*

#### CHALLENGE

Write one part of your story that inspires praise. Consider what might prevent you from sharing this with others.

#### REFLECTION

What was the last story you heard from someone else that inspired praise for God's goodness?
Why do you think stories of God's faithful work in the lives of His people are personally encouraging?

*Monday—Evening*

Praise is the choice to assign worth to God's involvement in every aspect of your life. When you believe God is worthy of your praise, worship, and adoration, you'll be more likely to consider Him willing and able to help when you need it. When God is considered most worthy, you'll find reason to show Him honor, respect, and trust.

*Dear God, when it comes to my attitude toward prayer, there's a connection between my willingness to praise You and my belief in the value of prayer. My praise honors You, but it helps me believe more completely in Your love for me. Thank You. Amen.*

**CHALLENGE**

Make a list of three specific areas of your life. Identify God's involvement in each area.

**REFLECTION**

What does it mean to you to assign worth to God? How can you do it?

How can seeing God as worthy improve your prayer life?

## *Week 6: Tuesday*

## *A* IS FOR ADMIT

*If we claim that we're free of sin, we're only fooling ourselves.
A claim like that is errant nonsense. On the other hand,
if we admit our sins—make a clean breast of them—he won't
let us down; he'll be true to himself. He'll forgive our sins and
purge us of all wrongdoing. If we claim that we've never
sinned, we out-and-out contradict God—make a liar out of
him. A claim like that only shows off our ignorance of God.*
1 JOHN 1:8–10 MSG

Prayer requires honesty (Proverbs 12:22). Honesty requires a sober assessment of who you are in Christ (Romans 12:3). A sober assessment means knowing that you are a sinner, and God loves sinners (Romans 5:8).

God's Word tells us in Romans 2:4, "In kindness [God] takes us firmly by the hand and leads us into a radical life-change" (MSG). Part of that life change is a new willingness to admit you've blown it. Admitting personal sin is the second part of the *PAGES of prayer model.*

It can be easy to think of any violation of God's rules as a mistake, lapse of judgment, or a deeply private choice, but sin always keeps you separated from God. The reset in your relationship with God is admitting you've sinned. Be transparent, specific, and honest.

When you refuse to admit your sin in prayer, you aren't fooling God. You can't act as if He doesn't already know you've violated His rules, trust, and plan. You're guilty. Admit it.

Accept His forgiveness—walk with God.

*Tuesday—Morning*

Admitting personal sin means knowing what sin is. You might sin and know you're a law breaker. You might sin and learn later that you broke God's rules. In either instance you can immediately come to God in prayer and admit your sin. No matter how hard you try, you will never be without the ability to sin. Keep the lines of communication open between you and God by accepting His life reset—forgiveness.

*Dear God, I don't want to be guilty of ignoring sin or treating it as if it isn't a big deal. I don't want to see how close I can get to sin without sinning. Keep me close and keep me coming back to You. Amen.*

### CHALLENGE

Describe a time when you decided not to admit your sin to God. Spend time remembering what you learned by keeping yourself away from God's forgiveness.

### REFLECTION

Have you ever believed there was a statute of limitations on the penalty for your sin? What impact does this thinking have on prayer?

Why is a closeness to God important to you?

*Tuesday—Noon*

When you become a Christian, your past sins are forgiven. You're given a fresh start, but sin is not treated like a preexisting condition on an insurance policy that obligates God to overlook new sin or excuse it because you're new to Christianity. Sin always places distance between you and God. Admitting every new sin reopens the lines of communication and initiates healing.

*Dear God, thank You for the gift of forgiveness. I'm overwhelmed that You made a way for me to come close when my own actions cause me to believe I have no right to expect You to accept my imperfection. Your Son, Jesus, made it possible to come to You and receive forgiveness. May shame never prevent me from coming home. Amen.*

### Challenge

Write down what you believe is the benefit of God's fresh start. Consider whether that information influences your willingness to admit personal sin.

### Reflection

As a person who sins, what response should you expect from God?

How important is forgiveness in keeping prayer a desirable part of your spiritual life?

## *Tuesday—Evening*

There is a reason for honesty in prayer. If sin offends God, then refusing to be honest compounds the impact of the sin that keeps you distant from God. When you admit your sin, it doesn't catch God by surprise. He already knows. Your honesty suggests your willingness to return to the life path He's prepared for you.

*Dear God, why do I ever try to hide my sin from You?*
*Why do I act as if nothing has happened and life can return*
*to normal? Maybe I have tried fooling others long enough*
*that I think I can fool You, too. Help me see that sin places*
*barriers in my relationships with others and places me*
*at a distance from Your forgiveness. Amen.*

### CHALLENGE

Write down ways you believe God can be fooled by withholding information about your sin.

### REFLECTION

Why do you think God wants you to be completely honest when you pray?

If God is not surprised by the sin in your life, why do you struggle with admitting personal sin?

# *G* IS FOR GRATITUDE

*Give thanks to the Lord, for he is good!*
*His faithful love endures forever.*
PSALM 136:1 NLT

Prayer can be a fresh expression every time you say, "Dear God." Gratitude makes the stale fresh. It's a response that indicates God's goodness has been noticed and valued. It suggests you wholeheartedly embrace the plan God is working to complete in your life.

Gratitude recognizes God's love, forgiveness, and faithfulness. It's the appropriate response to the infinite number of things God has done. It recognizes that the alternative to God's goodness is a long journey through *Doom Gulch and Trouble Turnpike.*

When you show gratitude to others an emotional link forms, because when you needed help someone helped you. Gratitude recognizes you can't do everything on your own, points to the need for community, and improves your ability to see and meet the needs of others.

It's possible to think God selfishly demands recognition for everything He does, but this thinking fails to comprehend how valuable gratitude is in enlarging the value of other people. There's a reason for everything that God asks of His family. What He asks is always for your benefit.

*G* is for gratitude and it's the third concept in the

*PAGES of prayer model.* God made this day. Be grateful (Psalm 118:24). God sends people into your life. Show gratitude in prayer (Ephesians 1:16). Every good gift is from God. Accept it with thanks (James 1:17). Thanksgiving is a sacrifice that honors God. Offer it (Psalm 50:23). You get to pray to God. Thank Him for the gift of communication (Psalm 118:28).

Pray grateful prayers.

## Wednesday—Morning

Expressing gratitude is one of the best ways to clarify value in the family of God. Expressing gratitude in prayer is the best way to remember God's goodness and believe that His work in your life is just what you need. Gratitude denies the need for competition and creates the opportunity to help and be helped.

*Dear God, gratitude is a mark of growth, a symbol of dependence on You, and a recognition that my best days bear the marks of a great God. Help me remember that the polite thing to say is "Thank You." The right thing is to mean it when I express gratitude to You. Amen.*

### CHALLENGE

List as many things as you can that God has done that inspire gratitude. Thank Him for each item and be as specific as you can about why you're grateful.

## REFLECTION

What's the difference between praise and gratitude? How are praise and gratitude similar?

## *Wednesday—Noon*

It's hard for someone who is self-sufficient to express gratitude. There is a sense that a self-sufficient person doesn't need or even want help. They might only accept help on the condition the help is repaid in some way. This mind-set doesn't work with the God who can do what you can't, and He doesn't accept your best effort as repayment for *gifts* like mercy, grace, and love.

> *Dear God, may I never try to barter for a slice of Your goodness. Help me remember what You offer to me is a gift I can't repay. When I work for You, may it be because I'm grateful and not because I feel some misguided obligation to work for Your gifts. Amen.*

## CHALLENGE

List the top three gifts God has given you. Consider what you think you would have to pay for those gifts. Does it make you grateful that God offered them to you as a gift?

## REFLECTION

Have you ever been overwhelmed with gratitude to God?
  What did you learn?
Why do you think God doesn't want you to take
  Him for granted?

## *Wednesday—Evening*

One of the primary reasons "gratitude" follows "admit personal sin" in the *PAGES of prayer model* is that once you've been given a renewed relationship with God through forgiveness, there should be no barriers to the expression of gratitude. Once gratitude is expressed, it will set the tone for the remainder of your prayer.

> *Dear God, I'm learning that You're more than worthy of every word of praise I can say. I'm learning that I sin, and admitting my faults to You brings me to Your courtyard of forgiveness, leaving me grateful. I am filled with joy spending time in Your presence. Amen.*

## CHALLENGE

Think of a time when someone gave you a gift that inspired immediate and sincere gratitude. Now, think of everything God has given you. Compare and contrast your level of gratitude in both cases.

### REFLECTION

When someone expresses gratitude for something you've done, does it make you feel closer or further away from that person? Why?

Would you say that gratitude invites greater relational intimacy? Explain.

# *E* IS FOR ENGAGED

*The earnest prayer of a righteous person has
great power and produces wonderful results.*
JAMES 5:16 NLT

Small children are often taught prayers that are simple and memorized. They recite these prayers before bed, at mealtimes, or in church.

As you grow, you learn that these prayers may provide comfort because they've been prayed so often, but they often lack the very thing that can bring you closer to God—personal engagement.

It's possible to settle for "to-do list" prayers that include all the right words while your mind and heart drift to faraway places. This is why many prayers uttered before bedtime result in sleep instead of answers.

A lack of engagement in prayer can actually lead you to think you've wasted your time. Oswald Chambers once wrote, "Prayer does not fit us for the greater work; prayer is the greater work." Pray, read God's Word, obey, and as you learn and respond, you're engaging in the process God uses to create a righteous person.

*E* is for engaged in the *PAGES of prayer model*. Prayer can't be effective if you're just going through the motions. The Bible contains many examples of engaged prayer warriors. Names include Job, Jeremiah, Hannah, Moses, and the psalmists. Even Jesus knew the value of engaged prayer. Luke 22:44 says, "He prayed more fervently, and he was in such agony of spirit that his sweat fell to the ground like great drops of blood" (NLT). It seems appropriate to use the words fervent, earnest, passionate, ardent, or even zealous to describe an engaged prayer, a difference-making prayer.

## Thursday—Morning

In the *PAGES of prayer model* (letter *E*) it makes sense to use a notebook to make a list of the things you want to pray about. Be intentional in your prayers. It's easy to lose your concentration and shift your thinking to other things that battle for your attention, but when you're solidly engaged in prayer, you're making and keeping an appointment with God. You *can* prepare for your meeting.

*Dear God, may my mind be sharp, my thinking clear, and our time sweet. I want my prayers to have focus. When I can, help me come to You with everything I need to speak with You. If I can't, please help me learn what I need to learn to move me to this kind of prayer. Thanks for loving me even when I struggle with how to speak to You. Amen.*

### CHALLENGE

Recall a time when a prayer seemed pointless. Consider how being engaged in your prayer life could improve your connection to God.

In your life, what word would you use to honestly
describe your experience in prayer (privilege,
responsibility, difficulty, etc.)?

What concept makes the most sense to you in today's
reading?

## *Thursday—Noon*

It's likely you find yourself able to engage well in certain
aspects of life. This could be sports, travel, cooking, or
video games. It's not that there isn't an understanding of
what engagement looks like. The real struggle is taking
what you know about engaging and applying it to prayer.
If you can internalize this idea, imagine the profound
impact it could have on your prayer life.

> *Dear God, why can I get excited about a game or a recipe
> but still find prayer less than inspiring? It should be more,
> but so often I feel lost in repeated words with no real sense of
> connection with You. Help me take what I'm learning and let
> my words come freely and intentionally to Your ears. Amen.*

### CHALLENGE

If you've thought about prayer as something you only
needed to do when you had a concern, how does this
connect with today's Bible verse and the quote from
Oswald Chambers?

## REFLECTION

Have you ever looked forward to praying with the same enthusiasm as you might the release of a new movie or phone? Why or why not?

Why do you think God pays attention to the prayers of the fervent?

## *Thursday—Evening*

An engaged prayer is one that understands that if you are going to get to the place God has in mind for you, then there needs to be conversation that really deals with issues, expresses gratitude, and is clear about the need for help. Pray that kind of prayer.

*Dear God, thank You for being passionate enough about me to rescue me from myself. I am grateful Your objective was clear enough that You intentionally offered hope when I was wrapped in a blanket of apathy and self-pity. Help me take the opportunity to pray with focus and passion. Amen.*

## CHALLENGE

Write a prayer that includes all elements of the *PAGES of prayer model* so far. Be intentionally engaged in the prayer. Write down your experience and note any changes you discovered when compared to past prayers.

## REFLECTION

Have you ever thought that a passionate prayer is
  disrespectful to God? How does today's materials
  challenge this thought?

Why do you think a passionate prayer is part of an
  abundant life?

## Week 6: Friday

# S IS FOR SEEKING GOD'S HELP

*Lord, I cry out to You; make haste to me!*
*Give ear to my voice when I cry out to You.*
PSALM 141:1 NKJV

David prayed some amazing prayers. Some petitioned God for help while others focused on praise. Some captured despair, others gratitude.

It's one of David's psalms that help highlight some practical points to personal prayer. *S* stands for seeking God's help in the final letter in the *PAGES of prayer model*.

Seeking God's help is for you and it's for everyone you know. It's a request that God step in where other plans have failed. Psalm 141 affirms that you should pray when you have a need.

Learn this. Pray in a way that pleases God (v. 2). Stay away from careless words in prayer (v. 3). Ask God to keep evil thoughts from invading your prayer life and spilling over into the everyday (v. 4). Tough words from faithful friends can be the positive outcome of prayer (v. 5). God is a fortress of kindness so concentrate on Him (v. 8). Pray for God's plan to win out over evil within society (v. 10).

Today's reading has focused on what adding prayers for yourself and others looks like from the perspective of David's prayer.

This is the final letter in the *PAGES of prayer model*, which means you now have five prime elements you can infuse into your prayers that should fuel improved communication with God. Put them together and share quality time with the One who made a friendship possible between the created and the Creator.

## *Friday—Morning*

Isaiah 55:6 says, "Seek GOD while he's here to be found, pray to him while he's close at hand" (MSG). Good news, He's always close at hand, so pray. Seek His will. Seek His help. Seek His blessing. Seek God for your needs, and the needs of those you know.

*Dear God, seeking You should be the desire of my heart.*
*Knowing You should be a sign of spiritual growth.*
*Loving You should be my perfect response to Your nearness.*
*When these things aren't true of me, remind me to seek,*
*know, and love You once more. Amen.*

### CHALLENGE

The Bible says that time is short (2 Corinthians 6:2) and humans are fragile (1 Peter 1:24). Consider whether it's reasonable for God to ask us to seek Him so we don't waste our time on failed ideas.

### REFLECTION

Why do some people refuse to seek God?
Why might you refuse to seek God even knowing He meets needs?

## Friday—Noon

God wants you to grow in your faith (Hebrews 6:1–2). You might think that means you *grow out* of your need for God's help. This idea is opposed to scripture. Seek God, cry out to Him, and call on His name. Be thankful you'll never outgrow your need for God.

*Dear God, when I think I'm big enough to handle pain and struggle on my own, may I express sorrow at my wrong thinking. Help me spend my time wisely by calling on You to help when I'm in trouble. Every time I pray, I have an opportunity to learn from You. May I be a willing student for the perfect Instructor. Amen.*

### CHALLENGE

Consider how it might help to think of your prayer life as part of course work in God's divine classroom. Consider how it helps to have complete access to the thoughts of the Instructor in the Bible.

### REFLECTION

Why do you think it's irresponsible to think of yourself as someone who can outgrow the need for God?

If you've thought that God only helps you if you help yourself, how does this idea fit with what you're learning?

## Friday—Evening

If you want to study the idea of seeking God more completely, you might begin a study of the Psalms and pinpoint the instances where the psalmists seek God and pray for His help, intervention, and guidance. The Psalms provide a divine billboard posting details about the only real source of strength when weakness has overstayed its welcome.

*Dear God, may my interest in prayer allow me to continue to learn long after this week ends. Thanks for including the Psalms in Your Word. I can learn from those who've struggled to understand before their need met Your willingness to help. Amen.*

### CHALLENGE

List at least one instance when you had no reasonable expectation that your troubles would lead to anything other than catastrophe, yet God showed up and you acknowledged His help. Remember in words how God's help impacted your life. Recall the response you had in the moment you realized God's answer to your crisis was mercy.

### REFLECTION

How might you be able to help others who are struggling to learn to seek God for answers?
In what ways does the *PAGES of prayer model* make sense to you? What part remains a struggle?

# BE A PAGE

*Looking unto Jesus, the author and finisher of
our faith, who for the joy that was set before Him
endured the cross, despising the shame, and has sat
down at the right hand of the throne of God.*
HEBREWS 12:2 NKJV

You've been introduced to the *PAGES of prayer model* this week. The acronym is a reminder of the value of prayer, how God answers prayer, and those who actually prayed.

You've been asked to use a notebook for the last six weeks, and in those *pages* you should have discovered through your own answers the incredible value of prayer. You've been asked to read the *pages* of God's Word because this is the primary source of God's answers to the questions you ask. When it comes to those who actually pray, you may be interested in knowing that the term "pages" is used to describe people engaged as personal attendants of an esteemed leader.

The *PAGES of prayer model* looks like this:

P – Praise God
A – Admit Personal Sin
G – Gratitude Expressed to a Great God
E – Engage in Prayer
S – Seek God's Help or Answer

You may be thought of as a *page* in one other sense. God is writing a story for the ages. The page of your story is included. He has not left you alone, and He'll never forsake His family (Deuteronomy 31:6).

God has invested so much in your future that it just makes sense to learn what that future is—and how to get there. This knowledge is available for the asking.

### Saturday—Morning

If you took advantage of answering questions in a notebook, look through your thoughts, questions, and answers. You may find that your thinking about prayer has changed. You might update what you've written or you may be reminded of something you want to study a bit more.

*Dear God, may I grow more comfortable with each prayer. May I seek Your Word with greater faithfulness. May I obey You with what I learn. May my life look more like Yours with each conversation. Amen.*

#### CHALLENGE

Compose a *PAGES prayer*. Offer it to God as an indication that you want to improve the level of communication between yourself and the God who made you.

Which part of the *PAGES of prayer model* seems the
   hardest for you? Why?
Which part do you like the most? Explain.

## *Saturday—Noon*

Prayer doesn't need to be reduced to a formula, but the
prayer plan we've looked at in our final week is a solid
reminder of things God has already indicated in His
Word are appropriate and welcome when you pray.

> *Dear God, I want to honor You in the way I talk to You*
> *and what I talk about. May I be quick to admit when I*
> *have not been faithful in following You. May my lips be*
> *free in thanking You. When my mind drifts, help me*
> *reengage in my prayer to You. I want Your answers.*
> *Help me to cooperate with Your plan. Amen.*

**CHALLENGE**

Write down the things you've been most encouraged to
try this week when praying to God.

**REFLECTION**

Do you think a prayer plan can help you in your prayer
   life? Explain.
What part of this week's readings have you spent the
   most time considering?

*Saturday—Evening*

God's Word brings light to dark thinking, hope to despairing hearts, and new life to those who thought existence was the best they could hope for. God's Word can answer prayers, bring clarity to wrong thinking, and offer a way when all you see ahead are roadblocks. God's Word and your prayer life are allies in the art of divine conversation.

*Dear God, learning Your Word can help me stop the spiritual small talk. Help me taste and see that Your Word is not only good but life changing. Transform my thinking and conform me to Your will. You have more than permission—You have my heart. Work in me, today. Amen.*

### CHALLENGE

Consider to what degree you are convinced that a radically transformed prayer life can alter your relationship with God. List the top three things you've learned that you believe can help.

### REFLECTION

Refer to pages 186–187 and the connections to the word "pages." What aspect do you connect with most?
Is prayer more or less important to you today than when you picked up this book? Why?

# CONCLUSION

*Don't pray when you feel like it. Have an appointment with the Lord and keep it. A man is powerful on his knees.*
CORRIE TEN BOOM

Forty-two days is the equivalent of 1,008 hours; 60,480 minutes; or 3,628,800 seconds. While that seems like a lot of time, it isn't nearly enough to tackle every aspect of a prayer life that can be powerful, effective, and offers lasting change.

You're at the end of a guided tour that encourages you to pick up where this book ends and walk on with a greater confidence in your personal conversations with God.

Beyond the *PAGES of prayer model* you should have a greater appreciation for the connection between your prayers and God's answers within the pages of the Bible.

He walks with you in tough times. His plan for your life is released as you grow in faith. His ability to speak to you is amplified by your ability to listen to Him.

Your notes should help you track the thoughts you had about prayer and allow you to track changes that took place in your thinking as you spent time in these pages.

Remember, you pray to a God who will never violate your trust, so speak freely. You address a God who created you for relationship and makes no distinction between people, so don't be intimidated. You can be friends with the God who created language, so use your words to honor Him.

You've been given a path forward in how to pray. It

has the potential to alter perspective, elevate confidence in prayer, and provide an understanding of the things God wants you to pray for.

There is no amount of *want to* that will automatically improve your prayer life. When God answers your prayer in scripture, you'll bear the responsibility of obedience to what you've learned. Sometimes God's answers look a lot like work but may be opportunities in disguise. God will answer your prayers in the way that best links His purpose and your response.

Refer back to this book if needed, but always refer to God's Word as an authoritative document that's filled with the words of life, love, and the promises of God.

As you close this book, remember prayer was created for you. It provides a direct line of communication with God that's available without reservation or restriction on its way to refining your character and renewing your spirit.

In this book about God, it's only right that His Word has the final say. "When I was desperate, I called out, and GOD got me out of a tight spot. GOD's angel sets up a circle of protection around us while we pray. Open your mouth and taste, open your eyes and see—how good GOD is. Blessed are you who run to him" (Psalm 34:6–8 MSG).

## ALSO AVAILABLE FROM BARBOUR BOOKS:

*1,001 Prayers to Energize Your Prayer Life*

Prayer is a powerful privilege given to Christians, but we often struggle to know where to start. Here, readers will find hundreds of uplifting and challenging prayer starters in *1,001 Prayers to Energize Your Prayer Life.* This compact book offers simple, heartfelt prayers for many of life's situations, and readers will find just the right pick-me-up for daily conversations with their heavenly Father.

Paperback / 978-1-68322-345-0 / $5.99